D0583389

JEWS AND THE
AMERICAN
RELIGIOUS
LANDSCAPE

JEWS AND
THE AMERICAN
RELIGIOUS
LANDSCAPE

UZI REBHUN

Columbia University Press   *New York*

Columbia University Press
Publishers Since 1893
New York   Chichester, West Sussex
cup.columbia.edu

Library of Congress Cataloging-in-Publication Data

Names: Rebhun, Uzi, author.
Title: Jews and the American religious landscape, Uzi Rebhun.
Description: New York : Columbia University Press [2016]
Includes bibliographical references and index.
Identifiers: LCCN *2016002656* I ISBN 9780231178266 (cloth : alk. paper) I
ISBN 9780231541497 (e-book)
Subjects: LCSH: Jews—United States—Social conditions. I Jews—
United States—Identity. I Judaism—United States—History—21st
century. I United States—Ethnic relations.
Classification: LCC E184.36.S65 R428 2016 I DDC 305.892/4073—dc23
LC record available at *http://lccn.loc.gov/202016002656*

c 10 9 8 7 6 5 4 3 2 1

JACKET DESIGN: NOAH ARLOW

CONTENTS

PREFACE

OR THE past twenty-five years, my scholarly work has focused on the demography and sociology of Jews, particularly American Jews. It has led me to the investigation of diverse topics within the American Jewish experience, including geographic dispersion and mobility, the Jewish family, Jewish identification, relations between American Jewry and Israel, the adjustment of Jewish immigrants to the United States, and projections on the future demographic evolution of American Jews. I have observed the fascinating dynamic and the rapid changes that this Diaspora community, the largest and also the most successful in modern Jewish history, has been undergoing. The guiding concept in my research is the idea that the social patterns of Jews can be assessed only in the context of American society at large, the individual's specific Jewish communal environment, his or her background and current characteristics, and the need to follow trends over time. This multidimensional comparative insight has exposed me to the complexity, and often the ambivalence, of the meandering trajectories that American Jews have been following. Consequently, I identify with neither of the unequivocal schools of thought that pertain to American Jewry—vitality on the one hand and twilight on the other.

To apply the aforementioned comparative approach, my studies investigate Jews in view of or in contrast with the American population at large (especially non-Hispanic whites) using National Jewish Population Surveys (NJPS) from 1970, 1990, and 2000/01 in conjunction with decennial censuses from the same years. I also utilize Jewish community surveys, e.g., of Boston, Philadelphia, and Los Angeles, to examine spatial variations and the role of place of residence as a determinant of Jewish identification. Yet another combination of data is between findings relating to American Jews and those pertaining to their Jewish peers in Israel; this integrated approach illuminates, among other things, similarities and dissimilarities in the structure and rhythm of religioethnic identification of Jews as minority and majority populations in their respective countries of residence. These surveys yield rich and uniform data on many characteristics of their interviewees.

Insofar as these sources allowed, I examined trends in my area of inquiry over a decade or two, interpreting "time"—the difference between a later period and an earlier one—as an immensely important dimension in understanding ideological, social, and cultural processes in the general scene of American society. Nevertheless, time is largely inclusive and penetrates individuals and various segments of the population.

My empirical infrastructure thus far, however, was deficient in an important way: it lacked data that would allow comparison between Jews and other defined religious groups across a wide array of religious indicators and major areas of life. I now have an opportunity to fill this gap, for the first time and possibly the only time for many years to come. The source of this opportunity is the 2007 Pew Religious Landscape Survey, comprised of tens of thousands of respondents, including enough Jews to permit quantitative analysis. The result is the present monograph, which observes and analyzes the social, religious, and political patterns of Jews from a comparative perspective that juxtaposes them to the contemporary American religious mosaic of members of the Christian majority, specific denominations within this majority, other religious minorities, and the nonreligious.

Although the major aim of the study is to take a new look at American Jews, its many observations also offer copious data for those interested in other religious or ethnic groups. Moreover, insights gleaned from the study of Jews are important in determining what may be expected among other American religious minorities. Previous studies suggest that American Jews have often been ahead of other religious and ethnic minorities (of European descent) in challenging the majority's demographic and sociocultural opportunities. To assess the prospects of integration among more recently arrived minority groups, one needs to examine in depth the path taken by previous groups. Only then can the elements of continuity and disjuncture between the experiences of veteran religious minorities and those of the present day be fairly evaluated. Thus, as we aim to learn about Jews from a broad comparative perspective, other religious groups may learn from the Jewish case to better understand themselves.

This research project was carried out in my academic home, the A. Harman Institute of Contemporary Jewry of the Hebrew University of Jerusalem. There Sergio DellaPergola, my mentor in graduate studies and an observer of my work ever since, also read parts of this manuscript and provided astute comments. I am also grateful to several colleagues in Israel or abroad, each of whom kindly read a chapter of this book and made valuable suggestions:

Yaacov Ariel, Harriet Hartman, Lawrence Kotler-Berkowitz, Eli Lederhendler, Bruce Phillips, Chaim I. Waxman, and Esther Wilder. I also wish to convey my appreciation to the Pew Forum for its long-lasting commitment to collecting data on religious and public life and presenting them to the public for use.

Finally, this book is dedicated to my wife, Maayan, and to our children, Eynat, Noa, and Ido, devoted partners in my scientific and intellectual journey to American Jewry, in which together we experienced Jewish life at different times and locations across the American continent.

Jerusalem, April 2014

JEWS AND THE
AMERICAN
RELIGIOUS
LANDSCAPE

INTRODUCTION

Religion in America

RELIGION IS central in American life for members of all social and economic strata. Even if its potency may have diminished somewhat in recent times, religion today is more diverse than ever, omnipresent in the public domain including culture and politics, pluralistic and embellished with new forms of beliefs and practices. Americans' religious identity is dynamic. People move freely among religious styles to maximize the meaning and role of religion and spirituality in their lives. Pluralism and individualism, however, also convey the possibility of challenging religion in the name of "Americanism" and turning toward secular worldviews (Bellah et al. 1996 [1985]; Campbell and Putnam 2010; Chaves 2011; Cohen and Numbers 2013; Eck 2001; Kosmin and Lachman 1993; Putnam 2000; Wuthnow 2004).

RELIGIOUS CHOICES

Affiliation with a religious denomination is immensely important in the United States; it evidences a commitment to the most exalted of American values and reflects full participation in civic life (Swatos 1981). Being part of a religion means "being American"—identifying with and positioning oneself in the American social structure (Greeley 1972). Thus religion provides Americans not only with meaning but also with a sense of belonging (Carroll and Roof 1993). Often, a religious denomination connects people to the community (Swatos 1981).

Americans manifest their religious preferences in a society that, notwithstanding certain challenges, honors the separation of religion and state as well as freedom of religion. Despite these characteristics, which are deeply rooted in American democracy, and despite the free market of religious alternatives, Protestantism—particularly in its modern mainline denominations—has long been the country's most durable and leading faith (Ahlstrom 1975; Hudson 1965; Marty 1986), the one that "set[s] the terms for the religious dimensions of empire" (Marty 1970:23). The American spiritual style attributes importance to the unity of, and adherence to, the minutiae of this grand theological or philosophical system (Roof 1993). Protestant Christianity established ethical norms and values that shaped American culture in literature, the arts, the theater, and scholarship. The Protestant ethic set the tone for public institutions and personal ways of life (as in the expression "Protestant culture"; Hollinger 1997). Insofar as this brand of Protestantism developed along pluralistic lines, it largely encouraged the proliferation of Protestant groups or churches, some liberal and others conservative, that recognize each other, respect each other, and, generally speaking, uphold the fundamental of freedom of choice (Greely 1972). Catholics, Jews, and African Americans, in contrast, often faced debilitating prejudices and social discrimination (Roof and McKinney 1987).

Indeed, immigrants to the U.S. in the late nineteenth and early twentieth centuries were expected to jettison almost everything they had brought from their birth countries and adopt the living patterns of their new home. This expectation, however, did not include the abandonment of the "old country" religion in favor of a mainstream American alternative. Immigrants were expected to preserve their old faiths to help them in finding a defined place in American life. In practice, they developed a somewhat ambivalent attitude toward these faiths, ranging from indifference to transition to more American denominations. Just the same, ties with the old faith were rarely severed totally. Accordingly, when mass immigration ended and a third generation emerged amid growing pluralism and abandonment of the conformity and melting pot ethos, a return to the parents' religion took place. The turn was a response to the horrors of World War II and an act of resistance to the threat of "godless" communism. There was no longer any reason to spurn religion; on the contrary, the immigrants' offspring wished to remember it. Religious affiliation became a leading trend in self-identity and social positioning for second-generation immigrants, and, in fact, for Americans at large, in the sense of Hansen's observation: "What the son wishes to forget the grandson wishes to remember" (Hansen 1938:9). Now, however, religious affiliation and its community and social contents seated themselves on a clearly visible tripod of Protestantism, Catholicism, and Judaism (Herberg 1983 [1955]; Sarna 2004).

In the 1960s, an era defined by dramatic events—the assassinations of the Kennedys and of Reverend Martin Luther King, the Vietnam War, and the civil rights struggle—the core religious cultures of the three large faith communities weakened. In their stead, a more pluralistic religious environment began to emerge, one populated by faiths including Islam, Buddhism, and Hinduism as well as atheism and agnosticism that had formerly been beyond the American religious pale (Perlmutter 1996). Old denominations (foremost Catholic) and new ones gathered strength pursuant to constitutional changes that opened doors, from 1965 on, to millions of migrants from Latin America, Eastern Asia, and Africa (Cohen and Numbers 2013; Evans 2013; Putnam 2000). Although these faiths had long been present in America, they have gained particular momentum in the past few decades in a process fraught with implications for American social and cultural life (Machacek 2003). Concurrently, evangelical Protestantism made proportionally large inroads, particularly among churchgoing Christians (Smidt 2013). Indeed, the evangelical renaissance may have been the most salient phenomenon in American denominational religious life in the second half of the twentieth century (Putnam 2000). This development reflects a characteristic of American history in which disciplined and less secular movements become institutionalized, yet exhibit an increasingly strong presence (Finke and Stark 1992).

Among white Protestants, it is important today to distinguish between liberals and conservatives as groups that have developed in contrasting directions (Hoge 1979; Roof 1993). The proportional growth of the conservative Protestant population relative to its liberal peers can be attributed to four main factors: higher fertility among conservatives, the deceleration of transitions from conservative denominations to liberal ones, less abandonment of the faith among young Protestant conservatives than among young liberals, and continued church membership among opponents of today's fast-moving changes in long-entrenched sexual mores and political attitudes. Thus conservative Protestantism owes its ascendancy mainly to more successful retention of members than the Protestant mainstream has been able to achieve

(Chaves 2011; Fischer and Hout 2006). This explanation is consistent with people's natural tendency to adopt unequivocal views and seek inflexible boundaries (Kelley 1972; Douglas 1984). The growth of the evangelical Protestant population, however, has not compensated for the thinning of mainline Protestantism, i.e., a decline in the total share of Protestants in the U.S. population (Chaves 2011; Putnam 2000). Protestantism is not alone in this development; in Catholicism, Judaism, and Islam, among other faiths, the fracturing into liberal and conservative camps has also been accelerating over time (Roof 1993), as is the tendency to abandon religion altogether (Fischer and Hout 2006; Greeley 1989; Putnam and Campbell 2010).

This era is also typified by more self-searching and religiosity by choice. These trends intermingle with a craving for new identities and the growth of spiritual leader-centered religious forms. The price for this is paid in the coin of congregational relations in which loyalty to traditional religious institutions, including those associated with specific denominations, has been undermined. Under these circumstances, religious groups compete with growing intensity for members, power, and influence (Roof and McKinney 1987). Religious denominations today take stands and act on current issues such as American foreign engagements, single-sex marriage, climate change, and social welfare, and individuals switch congregations more in accordance with their views on these topics than on the basis of their religious faith (Roof 1993). According to the rational-choice theory, people make decisions on religious affiliation in view of a simple cost-benefit analysis. This approach of self-choice also sheds light on the importance of the life cycle in influencing religious choices (Sherkat and Wilson 1995). Obviously, however, this construct cannot fully explain religious identity (Perl and Olson 2000). An alternative explanation proposes a cultural theory that takes account of a broader gamut of factors and the way they change over time. This theory emphasizes the effects of class and ascribed characteristics such as age, gender, and family background in determining religious preference (Loveland 2003; Woodhead 2007; Sherkat 2002). People who switch denominations tend toward the familiar and join the denominations that are closest to the ones that they have left (Babchuk and Whitt 1990), and, if no such denomination exists, they tend to forgo religious affiliation altogether (Sherkat 2000).

Formerly lily-white congregations, Catholic and Protestant alike, have also become ethnically and racially more diverse by admitting new members of African American, Hispanic, or Asian ethnicity (Chaves 2011). The Christian patterns practiced by recently landed immigrants may be very different from those of the religious institutions that they join; often the new members change the nature of the denominations (Machacek 2003). Not only is the U.S. becoming more diverse; families and social circles are increasingly composed of members of different religious extraction. As Putnam and Campbell (2010:5) note, "Nearly all Americans are acquainted with people of a different religious background . . . a co-worker, a close friend, a spouse, or a child." The upturn in religious diversity is accompanied by a cultural change manifested in an overall upturn in tolerance and appreciation of those of the other religious persuasion (Chaves 2011).

Thus the twentieth century was a time of steady increase in America's religious diversity. By its end, no country had more religious denominations than the U.S. The penetration of new faiths and the expansion of old and small ones signals the de-Europeanization of American Christianity (Warner 1998; Jenkins 2002). Today's American nation is, by and large, more democratic than before in that it accommodates more religious groups coexisting in religious tolerance and social equality (Eck 2001), indeed, some that may place their tenets over those of democracy. Furthermore, Americans switch faiths to an extent unequaled anywhere else (Kosmin and Keysar 2006).

RELIGIOUS PLURALISM

In accordance with the general social and cultural trends of postmodernism and postmaterialism, Americans' patterns of religious conduct are also noted for growing individualism. Most Americans consider religion a matter of personal choice that takes precedence over all organizational intervention (Bellah et al. 1996 [1985]). Many Americans adopt a religious system that blends elements of diverse traditions into something they consider personally appropriate and significant, tailoring faiths and spiritualities to fit their "size" and tastes. The resulting religion expresses a personal and sometimes eclectic choice that is characterized by multilayered styles of both beliefs and practices (Roof 1993). Each individual has his or her own version of religious reality (Roof and McKinney 1987). Consequently, people today are less similar to each other in their religious beliefs and mores.

Not only is religious belief open and diverse; sometimes it is unpredictable (Roof and McKinney 1987). Religious styles are dynamic, and people alter them over time, across life cycles, and when they change their place of residence. Religion constantly interacts with material culture, popular culture (books, music, films, advertising), social structure, and individuals' traits. Accordingly, it should be viewed as something that changes and lacks fundamental constancy (Christiano et al. 2008). Another factor behind the broad spectrum of options in religious patterns is the acceleration of integration among members of different ethnic and religious groups and the relaxation of external boundaries that once excluded certain groups from "America." Aberrations aside, Americans today, irrespective of their group affiliation, may reside in any neighborhood they like, attend the universities of their choice, work in occupations that interest them, and marry whomever they please (Horowitz 2003). Since religious activity is largely unrestricted in America, people can discover and celebrate faiths and values at any time, place, and manner of their choosing (Kosmin and Keysar 2006).

Given that a private religion is not a shared creed, it neither presses for strong group involvement nor even encourages it. What is more, religious autonomy sometimes claims a price in social commitment and community ties. Today's individualistic religion does not provide the support that a congregational affiliation imparts (Putnam 2000; Roof and McKinney 1987). One outcome of these developments is disengagement from houses of worship and official membership in religious institutions. Under such circumstances, the authority of religious leaders has lost much ground (Christiano et al. 2008). There has been an efflorescence of informal practices, aided in part by advanced computer technology, through which people create personal manifestations of religiosity and share them with others (Chaves 2011). Such a religion does not confine itself to the home; it permeates many geographic and social spaces such as workplaces, volunteer centers, and interfaith relations (Carroll 2013). Accordingly, one cannot assess a private religion by studying churches and participation in services only (Wuthnow 2004).

Still other Americans continue to belong to a congregation and attempt to redesign it in a way that would account for cultural changes and articulate their personal religious and moral needs. They can do this because most American religious institutions (like American institutions at large) are flexible and willing to accept and adjust to cultural changes. In congregations that have such members, the link with the religious denomination weakens. This powerful transformation, however, is not typical of the entire religious scene. Many Americans continue to embrace a traditional manner of conduct anchored in organized congregations that adhere to tried and unequivocal religious practices (Chaves 2011; Roof 1993).

Disengagement from churches and other religious congregations has social implications. The decline of congregational involvement has also diminished involvement in secular organizations, attenuated political involvement, and inhibited volunteering and assistance to others. A private religion may fulfill personal religious and even physical needs but reduces social capital. Accordingly, religious pluralism is having an identifiable chain effect that challenges community ties and, in turn, vitiates civil commitment (Chaves 2011; Putnam 2000). The weakening of religion in the public domain has also sapped religion's strength as a unifying force in American society. Religious subjectivity, however, broadens the boundaries of the country's moral discourse and enhances tolerance of religious differences (Cohen and Numbers 2013; Roof and McKinney 1987).

Religious pluralism also expands the supply of religious goods and services. The number of suppliers and their ability to efficiently produce and offer patterns of religious and spiritual beliefs are unlimited (Roof 1993). Thus today's American public domain abounds with players who compete intensively for potential consumers' hearts (Kosmin and Keysar 2006).

TRENDS IN AMERICAN
RELIGIOUS LIFE

The question whether proliferation of religious denominations and pluralism is amplifying religious vitality or weakening it is disputed (Chaves and Gorski 2001). Nevertheless, it is
widely agreed that both religious faith and activity in America,
by every global standard, are strong (Chaves 2011; Christiano et
al. 2008), notwithstanding a recent slight retreat (Putnam 2000).
Even many who turn their backs on institutional religion and
congregational and social commitment continue to express the
importance of religion in their personal lives (Roof 1993). Among
the religiously active, no few exhibit this in different ways than
before. Attending formal religious services in a house of worship
is no longer the only way of expressing group identity and commitment. Old patterns and beliefs sometimes yield to spiritual
experimentation and individual manifestations of religion and
faith (Roof and McKinney 1987). In a nutshell, American ways of
relating to religion are changing (Kosmin and Keysar 2006).

Two clashing processes have come into sight in the U.S. in
recent times: the religious majority is more intensely committed
to its creed, but more and more Americans are opting out of religion altogether (Kosmin and Keysar 2006). If so, Americans are
profoundly religious and profoundly secular (Roof and McKinney
1987). In today's era of postsecularism, religious and secular
worldviews may coexist and even engage each other in dialogue
(Habermas 2006). Admittedly, the average amount of time that
Americans devote to religious affairs, e.g., worship and social
activities in religious contexts, contracted by about one-third in
the last three decades of the twentieth century. This, however, is

mainly a result of the decline in the proportion of the population that devotes some time to religious affairs (Putnam 2000) with each generation being less active religiously than its predecessor. This distinction recurs when account is taken of the stage in the individual's life cycle. Thus baby boomers are less involved religiously than their parents were at the same age, and members of the postboomer generation slipped even more (Wuthnow 2007). Therefore, each time a generation passes on, the average level of American religiosity falls.

This tableau recurs not only from a generational point of view. Some Americans have distanced themselves from active involvement in religious communities; others are as involved as ever. The proportion of Americans who have totally disengaged from organized religious activity has grown; the share of those intensively involved in such activity has been stable. Consequently, dropouts come from the population whose involvement was moderate and expressed in traditional ways. The result is an increasing polarization—those who still adhere to tradition versus those totally unconnected with a religious congregation and a house of worship (Campbell and Putnam 2010). This polarization largely corresponds to the geographic dichotomy between the Northeast, typified by distancing from the faith, and the Bible Belt in the South, where these processes are much milder (Putnam 2000). The participation of Catholics in religious rituals has decreased markedly (Fischer and Hout 2006), whereas that of Protestants has been steady even though the ranks of Protestants have thinned; this is chiefly due to the ascendancy of evangelical congregations. More and more Catholics are becoming nominal members of the church, whereas many Protestants, as well as Jews, are putting all religious identity behind them (Putnam 2000). The long-term result is that religious people are becoming more different in their religious affiliation but more similar in their level of religious faith (Fischer and Hout 2006).

Tracking main indicators across the second half of the twentieth century reveals that religion gained a great deal of strength at first, particularly in the 1950s, and lost ground in the next two decades. At the turn of the twenty-first century, another slight retreat occurred, at least in terms of traditional patterns of participation in religious rituals. Thus the postwar religious upsurge waned (Putnam 2000). Recently, levels of religiosity—including beliefs, attitudes, and practices—have maintained overall continuity and, perhaps, a slight decline, but no pattern of religious activity has gained strength (Chaves 2011; Fischer and Hout 2006). If religion appears to be stronger than it used to be, this is only because it has become more closely associated with politics and social conservatism. Namely, religious matters are making more forceful inroads in the public discourse, and more people are engaging in or responding to them (Casanova 2001; Roof and McKinney 1987). The massiveness of today's houses of worship may also explain the greater prominence of religion (Chaves 2011).

The decline in religious involvement we have described is typical of whites and African Americans alike. Participation in worship services between the mid-1970s and the mid-1990s contracted similarly among members of both groups. The loss of church membership was slightly greater among African Americans. Still, they are more religious than whites (Putnam 2000).

JEWS IN AMERICA

Jews are one of the tiles in the American ethnoreligious human mosaic. Many American Jews today are two or three generations removed from the great mass of East European immigrants from the late nineteenth century. After those immigrants' arrival, they maintained strong social and cultural separatism, either willingly or due to discrimination. Their descendants in the second half of the twentieth century, however, enjoyed extraordinary integration and attained social and economic mobility. Jews today are concentrated in the upper tiers of schooling and white-collar occupations, hold key positions in politics, and stand out in the national media and mainstream culture (Burstein 2007; Chiswick 2007; Chua and Rubenfeld 2014; Davidson and Pyle 2011; Lipset and Raab 1995; Sklare 1978; Pyle 2006; Wilder 1996). Thus their contribution to the greatness of the U.S. is preeminent (Alba 2006; Ginsberg 2001).

These processes tie into general changes in American society—the substantial ebbing of stereotypes and prejudices about Jews, a downturn in discrimination, and the almost total disappearance of anti-Semitism in public life (ADL 2013; Chanes 1999; Kaplan 2005; Kosmin 2014; Perlman and Waldinger 1997; Shapiro 1992; Wistrich 2010). Amid these processes, Jews have strengthened their contacts with members of the non-Jewish American majority in college, on the job, and, as a result, in informal social networks (Kadushin et al. 2012). These contacts often create intimate friendships that lead to high rates of intermarriage (DellaPergola 2009; Pew 2013). The environment in which Jews operate exposes them to social and political trends that are characterized, at least in part, by an ethos of individualism and voluntarism (Cohen 1983; Liebman 1989; Madsen 2009).

The Jews' successful integration into and full acceptance by the general environment creates tension between them and their group identity, promoting "a shift from integration to survivalism" (Cohen 2003:1). Frequent contacts with people of the majority religion fray relations among Jews, loosen their ties with Jewish institutions, and distance them from particularistic religious and ethnic behaviors (Cohen 2012; DellaPergola 1991). The ultimate expression of the unraveling of a Jewish lifestyle is intermarriage. Those who marry non-Jews clearly exhibit a lower level of Jewishness than peers who marry Jews, even if demographic and socioeconomic differences between the groups are taken into account (Hartman and Sheskin 2012; Medding et al. 1992; Rebhun 1999). These processes do not necessarily lead to the disappearance of an identifiable American Jewry, since the Jews are not swapping their ethnoreligious identity for another one. More and more American Jews, however, are gradually developing an identity and self-image that blur their specificity vis-à-vis other Americans and emphasize their disengagement from traditional Judaism and from Jews in communities outside the United States. Thus an American Jewish identity is evolving (Seltzer and Cohen 1995) and incorporating itself into the domestic ethnic mosaic— an identity that is significantly differentiated—in beliefs and behavior—from the quondam Jewish identity (Alba 2006; Heilman 1995; Liebman 1989; "coalescence" of American and Jewish cultures; Fishman 2000).

Various indicators of identity and behaviors attest to the weakening of ethnoreligious orientations among American Jews. Follow-up over time reveals a decrease in the proportion of Jews who identify with any of the three main denominations of American Judaism—Orthodox, Conservative, Reform— and, concurrently, an increase in the share of those who express no denominational preference (Ament 2005; Kaplan 2009; Rebhun 1993). According to the secularization-modernization thesis, nonaffiliation with any main denomination is the last stop before total assimilation (Goldscheider 1986). Similarly, fewer

Jews of the baby boomer generation, relative to their pre–World War II-generation parents, state that it is very important for them to be Jewish (Waxman 2001). An intergenerational comparison of synagogue membership, frequency of synagogue attendance, Jewish philanthropy, belonging to informal Jewish networks, and residence in a neighborhood with a large Jewish presence, reveals less incidence among the young than among the older, and a gradual decline commensurate with age (Cohen 2005; DellaPergola 1991; Rebhun 2004).

According to this pessimistic approach, American Jews are vanishing. This is mostly manifested in high intermarriage rates and slackening commitment to Jewish community institutions. To wit, Jewish particularity vis-à-vis other religious and ethnic groups in practices and lifestyles is dissipating as the Jews steadily blend into the general society (Dershowitz 1997).

A different and more optimistic approach, however, asserts that even if stimuli for the abandonment of Jewish traditional and religious patterns exist, they are balanced out by new alternatives that are infusing the American Jewish culture with vigor and creativity (Freedman 2000; Goldscheider 2004; Horowitz 2003; Sasson, Kadushin, and Saxe 2010). According to this view, American Jews have adapted their cultural and religious behavior patterns to the reality of life in the surrounding modern society by redesigning a variety of forms, symbols, and institutions as minimum essential components of group identity and cohesion. As evidence, it suffices to observe the schedule of activities of any Jewish congregation, which replaces some of the erstwhile public religious rituals with lectures, fairs, and rituals for special events such as Holocaust Remembrance Day and Israel Independence Day. The growing importance of Holocaust awareness as a meaningful aspect of Jewishness (Rapaport 2005), especially in view of the destruction of European Jewry, also helps to demarcate American Jews from their general surroundings (Cohen 1999). Postmemories about the Holocaust include identity narratives of young adults who may not be the offspring of Holocaust survivors (Kaufman 2007), as nourished by organized tours to Eastern Europe, among other things (Aviv and Shneer 2007). Additional institutional connections and social contacts are unrelated to synagogues; they are associated with schools, libraries, and senior residences. Many Jews use Jewish community center facilities, partake in sports with other Jews, and so on (Goldscheider 2004). A major innovation was the development of spiritual communities by the Jewish renewal and *havurah* movements, which tailored religious practices to personal needs by offering cultural activities in folk craft, music, and dance, creative readings of religious texts, and (left-wing) politics (Kaplan 2005; Prell 1989). Indeed, although American Jews are experiencing structural and cultural changes that may reflect influences of prevalent general Western norms, these cannot undermine or lessen the vitality of Jewish social networks and family settings, which will continue to provide underpinnings for American Jewish vitality. Today, in a departure from the past, American Jews share many secular cultural patterns and religious manifestations that nourish one another and promote community cohesion (Goldscheider 2004, 2010; Goldscheider and Zuckerman 1984).

These new patterns furnish opportunities for the expression of group commitment at fixed times in the Jewish calendar (Etzioni 2004). Other opportunities crop up at specific stages of the life cycle; their degree of importance depends on changing circumstances relating to family, place of residence, and exposure to a Jewish environment. Although various kinds of evidence point to assimilation, and, in particular, decline in the observance of religious rituals and several aspects of community activity, the decrease is related mainly to the family life cycle. Ultimately, Jewish married young adults who have school-age children at home display a Jewish commitment that is no weaker than the one evinced by members of the previous generation when they were the same age, under similar family circumstances (Goldscheider 1986; Geffen Mintz 2005; Silberman 1985).

The growing extent of intermarriage is also related somewhat to personal background: an especially large proportion of Jews who maintain out-of-group family ties emerged from a weak Jewish background and received less socialization in the traditional Jewish value system. Thus, although the intermarried are less Jewishly involved than those who marry Jews, the former probably maneuvered along the fringes of Jewish life before they married as well (Cohen 1988; Lazerwitz et al. 1998; Phillips 2005). Moreover, when religiously differentiated spouses negotiate over their families' religious style, they may at times reinforce the awareness of group affiliation as a response to the partner's different religious identity (Fishman 2004). Generally speaking, a rather large share of exogamous couples maintains some connection with the Jewish people and Jewish rituals; these couples are also involved—admittedly, less intensively than endogamous couples—in organized Jewish activity (Goldscheider 2004). Many intermarried couples practice Jewishness in ways that rather closely resemble those of endogamous couples and are deeply concerned about maintaining Jewish connections and communal involvement (Dashefsky and Heller 2008; Thompson 2014). This is especially conspicuous among intermarried spouses who choose to raise their children as Jews (Gan et al. 2008). From the standpoint of the Jewish collective, intermarriage has limited meanings and may even be considered salutary in that it doubles the number of households that have at least one Jewish member. Thus only half the level of an endogamous couple's identification is needed to preserve Jewish identity. In sum, given its varied outcomes—some of which cancel each other out—intermarriage does not pose a serious threat to the Jewish continuity of much of American Jewry (Cohen 1995).

Another important determinant of Jewish continuity is the standing of Jews in society at large. The Jews' upward dispersion has redrawn their concentration in specific areas of residence, schools, and workplaces in a way that distinguishes them from other Americans in the sense of their acute structural homogeneity. This profile not only encourages Jews to interrelate more intensively; it also strengthens Jewish harmony and cohesion by encouraging commonalities of economic interests, social values, cultural styles, and even political goals (Chiswick 2014; Cohen 1983; Goldscheider 2004; Rebhun 2011). In fact, the Jews' social and economic achievements have freed them from concern about, and the need to strive for, integration into the mainstream; this allows them to start channeling their efforts in the additional direction of cultivating Jewish ethnic and cultural particularity (Brodkin 1998; Goldstein 2006).

A third and somewhat ambivalent interpretation of the trends in Jewish identification differentiates between ongoing ethnoreligious patterns and intermittent behaviors (Cohen 1998, 2003; Gans 1994; Rebhun 2004). While daily activities and official commitments have abated, those carried out on important festivals or on some other occasional basis, rituals observed in the home, and consciousness of the importance of being Jewish have remained largely stable. American Jews are shifting their loyalties from the public domain to the private one in what Cohen (2003:6) calls a "personalist shift," a change that has outcomes of less intensive ethnoreligious life and weaker community cohesion (Cohen and Eisen 2000). The emphasis on personal identity is further strengthened by advanced technology and the new opportunities that it offers for the acquisition of information about Judaism, the maintenance of contact with faraway relatives and friends, and the importation of Judaism into the home (Cohen 2012; Goldscheider 2004; Shandler 2009; Sheskin and Linen 2015). In addition, America today turns out an abundance of books and courses on Jewish themes, foremost the Holocaust (Horowitz 2011). From the subjective individual point of view, these personal identificational patterns are authentic and reaffirm the inherent connections of personal and group identity (Rebhun 2004). Interestingly, Jews are making more and more use of Yiddish and Hebrew words and expressions in their relations with other Jews. This use of particularistic linguistic markers is often a conscious act of identity that coexists with other symbolic practices that may not be intensively religious (Bunin, Benor, and Cohen 2011). Indeed, these trends are evident in particular among nonreligious Jews. Among the religious (the Orthodox and, to some extent, the Conservative), who identify strongly with their Jewishness, group identification, especially that of a religious nature, is on the rise. At the level of the individual self, then, some Jews are opting for much more America and much less Judaism, others are making the opposite choice, and yet others are seeking new forms of integration between the American and Jewish parts of themselves (Eisen 2007:106). If so, American Jewry, too, is evolving in diffuse directions (Cohen 2006; Himmelfarb and Loar 1984; Woocher 2005), with "a core . . . oriented around religion and a periphery clinging to the eroding remnants of ethnicity" (Freedman 2000:339). These two components of identification—religion and ethnicity—exist in a symbiosis that leaves one weak and the other strong (Sharot 2011).

It is also important to bear in mind that American Jews have been extraordinarily successful in achieving their collective goals, e.g., influencing American foreign policy on behalf of Jewish interests (Israel, Soviet Jewry), establishing a Jewish feminist movement, and expanding Jewish education in its various forms. These developments, reinforced by Jewish philanthropy and endowments in the billions of dollars, attest to a vital and committed Jewish community (Cohen 2003).

If so, at the beginning of the twenty-first century, American Jews enjoy autonomy in choosing among the main components of their group identification (Cohen and Eisen 2000). This refashioning of Jewish identification is an ongoing journey of inquiry and evolution, puzzlement and discovery, and the tailoring of customs to a Jewish lifestyle that will be meaningful to the individuals involved (Horowitz 2003). The result is the concurrent development of trends that often clash (Sarna 2004). As Kosmin postulated after taking a first glance at the 2013 Pew Research Center survey of U.S. Jews, "We should expect a growing diversity if not polarization among Jews as they increasingly seek to differentiate themselves among lifestyles, cultural, and political spectra" (2014:62). Complex and inconsistent behavior patterns such as these fuel a debate over the nature of Jewish identification in American society—a discussion involving, among other things, perceptions of erosion, awakening, and transformation (DellaPergola 2014a; Dutwin, Ben Porath, and Miller 2014; Saxe, Tighe, and Boxer 2014). In light of their structural characteristics and lofty social status, the Jews' group commitment is affected by general American ethnoreligious trends. Accordingly, this commitment should be assessed and understood in comparison with patterns among their peers in the Christian majority, specific denominations within this majority, and other religious minorities.

THE PEW SURVEY

The data for this study were culled from the 2007 Religious Landscape Survey (RLS), sponsored by the Pew Forum on Religion and Public Life (Pew Forum 2008). The RLS, conducted by Princeton Survey Research Associated International, included telephone interviews with a nationally representative sample of 35,556 adults living in households across the continental United States. The overwhelming majority of respondents (35,009) was reached through standard-list-assisted random-digit-dialed (RDD) telephone interviews.

Approximately ten attempts to contact a sampled telephone number were made. The calls were spread over times of day and days of the week to maximize the chance of contacting potential respondents. In each contact household, interviewers asked to speak with the youngest adult male presently at home. If no male was available, the second request was for the youngest adult female at home. This selection technique produced a sample that closely resembled the population by age and gender. Respondents could choose to be interviewed either in English or Spanish. The interviews took place between May 8 and August 13, 2007.

Notably, some five hundred interviews were completed with "cell phone only" respondents. Analysis of the data revealed no significant differences in religious makeup between this group and the sample of respondents from landline households. Thus the cell phone only respondents were excluded from the RLS dataset.

The present analysis concerns itself with respondents who belong to ten major religious groups, or an agglomerate of several small religions, in the United States. To a large extent, these religious tradition categories correspond to those used in the RLS reports. These groups include evangelical Protestants (N = 9,472), mainline Protestants (N = 7,470), historically black Protestants (or black Protestants) (N = 1,995), Catholics (N = 8,054), Mormons (N = 581), other Christians (N = 707), Jews (N = 781), Muslims (N = 116), affiliates of other faiths (1,159), and the unaffiliated (4,949). This focus elicited an overall sample of 35,284 respondents. The data were weighted for major demographic parameters including age, sex, education, race, region, nativity, and population density.

PLAN OF THIS BOOK

This study is set within the broader context of religion in America. It focuses on the Jews and attempts to analyze their behavior patterns at various complementary levels in comparison with those of affiliates of other faiths. The analysis yields insights both on the uniquenesses of the Jews and on their similarities with others and, accordingly—on fundamental processes of integration, separatism, and group boundaries. The comparative nature of the study also sheds light on the evolution of other major religious groups—Christian and non-Christian—that combine to shape the religious identity of contemporary America. Although the study relies on data from a single point of time, it emphasizes differences in age that reflect intergenerational trends, among other things, and differences in major personal characteristics such as gender, geography, and education.

The remainder of the book is composed of five chapters, each analyzing the Pew Survey data in regard to a different domain. By and large, each chapter sets the stage for the one that follows, yielding a comprehensive analysis of the issues discussed. The epilogue proposes and discusses several synthetic conclusions. Chapter 1 focuses on the size of the religious groups (including long-term changes in the major religious denominations) and the components of demographic changes—fertility, international migration, and religious switching. Here the age structure of each religious group is also observed, a factor that, while being an outcome of the group's demographic patterns, also may signal future changes in the American interreligious demographic equilibrium. Chapter 2 concerns itself with three main indicators of stratification: geographic dispersion (across the four major U.S. regions and by distinction among urban, suburban, and rural settlements), education, and earnings. For each religious group, the distribution of these stratification indicators are explored as well as the relations between these indicators and main sociodemographic characteristics. A multivariate analysis introduces Jews' group affiliation versus non-Jews and further decomposes the latter by detailed religious affiliation, as explanatory factors in the social and economic patterns observed. Chapter 3 calls attention to interfaith marriage by presenting data on its prevalence and the religious composition of the mixed couples. The geographic, educational, and economic characteristics are now incorporated into the demographic variables in an attempt to assess whether and to what extent group affiliation is a significant determinant of marital exogamy, all other things being equal.

Chapter 4 analyzes religious and ethnic identification. Its concern is with a broad range of life patterns—attitudes and behaviors in both the private and public spheres—that are relevant for Jews and for other religious groups. To that end, the data are treated from several different but complementary approaches, including an analysis of the structure of ethnoreligious identification, descriptive analysis of the strength of this identification, and an analysis of the determinants of group identification. Here marital status in general and its religious composition in particular are presented as an explanatory factor. The last empirical chapter—chapter 5—discusses political preferences. The Jews' liberal political leanings are well known and well documented; the chapter begins by offering explanations for this, some related to Jewish history, Jewish values, social stratification, and political interests. The chapter also reviews the voting patterns of Jews in the twentieth and early twenty-first centuries, with emphasis on the 2004 presidential race between George W. Bush and John (Forbes) Kerry—the last campaign before the data for this study were collected. To complete the analysis, the indicators of religioethnic identification from the previous chapter are inserted into the matrix of factors to explain differences between Jews and non-Jews in political orientation.

Each empirical chapter concludes with a summary of its main findings. The epilogue synthesizes the analyses and discusses the meanings of the observations in terms of the Jews' vitality and particularity. En passant, it also glances at the American religious scene at large.

1

POPULATION SIZE
AND DYNAMICS

RELIGION AND DEMOGRAPHY

RELIGION AND demography are strongly interrelated. Religious affiliation influences demographic patterns of fertility, mortality, and migration. Religion figures importantly in the pace and trajectory of demographic changes not only directly but also indirectly, through its effect on intervening factors such as age at marriage and family stability. Likewise, denominational preference, or the nature of group belonging, be it religious or ethnic, irrespective of the extent of religious involvement and practice, may attest to an individual's willingness to heed religious rituals, including those that aim to influence demographic fundamentals. Accordingly, in religiously diverse societies such as that of the United States, religious groups are experiencing unique changes in their size and, in turn, their share in the general population and their structural characteristics (Ebaugh 2003; Hout 2003; Hout, Greeley, and Wilde 2001; Mueller and Lane 1972; Park and Reimer 2002; Roof and McKinney 1987; Weber 1991 [1922]).

At times, religious groups remain stable even though they exhibit high or low levels of the demographic patterns that determine pace of growth. This may allude to another factor that affects group size: accession to or secession from the group. In a society that emphasizes principles of pluralism and individualism and has high rates of interfaith marriage, religious switching has a strong effect. Thus religious changes mirror broader social and cultural processes and are part of the American way of life (Emerson and Essenburg 2013; Schwadel 2013).

This chapter exploits a broad range of data from the 2007 Pew survey to analyze and discuss the demographic characteristics of American Jewry per se and in comparison with the patterns of other religious groups. Also, where possible, changes over the past fifty years are tracked with the help of data from the 1957 Current Population Survey. The issues discussed are population size, fertility, international migration, religious switching, and age composition.

POPULATION SIZE

The size of a religious group, i.e., the number of people who identify as belonging to a specific religion, is of prime importance in determining the group's visibility in the general environment, its social and political power, and its demographic patterns of fertility, mortality, migration, and identity changes (accession/secession). Occasionally, a group may be small in number but will stand out if characterized by high social and economic attainments by which it is situated at a major crossroads of the society at large. That exception aside, the size of a group is important in intergroup relations on the national scene and in the planning of the group's own community institutions and educational, cultural, and religious services. If members of a group share their religious faith with peers elsewhere, size will affect transnational relations, distribution of resources, and competition over center and periphery—all of which are carrying heavy ideological loads.

Much sociodemographic research on contemporary Jewry tends to define as Jewish all people who identify themselves as such, whether they consider their connection with Judaism religious, ethnic, or cultural, along with people of Jewish origin who express no religious preference. This group also embraces Jews by choice, i.e., those who adopt Judaism via formal conversion or otherwise. This highly inclusive approach is more reflective of subjective feelings rather than of rabbinic or any other legal definitions. It accepts a person as Jewish regardless of her or his commitment or behavior in terms of religiosity, beliefs, familiarity with Jewish sources, communal ties, and so on. This collective, known in the literature as the "core Jewish population," is the estimated pool for determining the size and characteristics of the Jewish population (DellaPergola 2014a; Kosmin et al. 1991).

The National Jewish Population Survey (NJPS), carried out in 2000/01, estimated the core Jewish population at 5.2 million persons (Kotler-Berkowitz et al. 2003). Some social scientists and community professionals criticized the NJPS for not having sampled the target population comprehensively, especially among those somewhat removed from Jewish involvement and commitment; for partial loss of survey-related information at an early screening stage; for a high nonresponse rate; and for counting as Jews some one million persons whose relation to Judaism is questionable, i.e., who reported having a Jewish background but were currently affiliated with a religion other than Judaism, provided it is not a competing faith (i.e., nonmonotheistic) faith (Kadushin,

Phillips, and Saxe 2005). This new estimate, however, was found to be highly compatible with the number of American Jews found in the previous NJPS from 1990 along the assumptions of continuity in demographic patterns and the large-scale emigration of Jews from the Soviet Union (DellaPergola 2005). Using this as a basis for yearly updating of the evolution of the Jewish population, and after upwardly correcting the original NJPS estimates for some undercounts, it was suggested that at the end of 2007 there were about 5.4 million Jews living in the United States (DellaPergola 2013a).[1]

Another way of estimating the size of American Jewry is by compiling local Jewish community surveys and tallying the results to yield a nationwide profile. This approach suffers from differences in the timing of the surveys (raising the risk of the double-counting of people who moved between communities) and inconsistency in defining the target population and in sampling techniques. Since not all Jewish communities have carried out a survey—this is said especially of small and isolated communities—their size can only be estimated on the basis of nonsurvey sources of unclear credibility. Based on such an approach, the number of Jews in America toward the end of the first decade of this century was estimated at 6.4 million (Sheskin and Dashefsky 2008). Still others employ a meta-analysis approach of general social surveys that include a question about religious faith and integrate these samples to form an estimate of the number of Jews in the country (Tighe et al. 2010). This method is susceptible to impediments similar to those of the community Jewish surveys: variations in timing of the data collection and different wording of questions about religious identity. Further, the general surveys do not ask about nonreligious types of belonging and therefore omit persons who identify only ethnically as Jews. These drawbacks, along with very small sample size (several dozen Jews in any given survey), create the risk of skewing the results severely. The combining of many surveys to obtain a large total sample does not necessarily surmount the separate biases of each survey. Moreover, these surveys concern themselves with adults only; they base the estimate of children (and of Jews not by religion) on other sources and assumptions. The meta-analysis elicits a population of approximately 6.5 million Jews in the United States in recent years (Saxe, Tighe, and Boxer 2014).

The difference between the lowest and the highest estimates, about one million people, is definitely meaningful. It may be resolved, reliably if not totally, with the help of the 2007 Pew survey. An analysis of the data (weighted) found 1,515 respondents who, when asked "What is your present religion, if any?" answered "Judaism" (hereafter "Jews by religion") and 261 respondents who professed no affiliation with any religion but indicated that one of their parents is Jewish (hereafter "ethnic Jews"). The tally yields 1,776 Jews out of the total of 88,292 respondents or 2.0115 percent. It must be remembered that only people aged eighteen and above took the survey.[2]

In 2007 the country had 301,621,000 inhabitants (U.S. Census Bureau 2008). Among them, 227,719,000 were adults aged eighteen and over (75.5 percent). Multiplying this number of adults by the percentage of Jews (227,719,000*2.0115/100), one obtains an adult Jewish population of 4,580,000 that year.

A Jewish population projection from 2000, based on that year's NJPS (which assumed the persistence of the recently prevailing levels of demographic factors), estimated the zero to seventeen age group in 2005 at 19.5 percent of the total Jewish population (half a percentage point lower than their share in 2000). There is no reason to believe that this proportion changed dramatically between then and 2007. Hence the U.S. Jewish population in 2007 may be estimated at 5,690,146 (4,580,568/80.5* 100). Obviously, any other assumption regarding the proportion of children would decrease or increase the total number of American Jews.[3]

To put it more conveniently, the sundry estimates of American Jewry range from a minimum of 5.4 million to a maximum of 6.5 million. The Pew survey finding, 5.7 million, falls into the lower half of the range. Given the many complexities that poll-takers face when measuring a rare population, and the sampling errors that characterize any sample-based survey, it may be useful to suggest not a fixed number of the American Jewish population but rather a range of 5.5 million to 6 million toward the end of the first decade of the twenty-first century. No less important is the observation that, apart from minor fluctuations, the number of American Jews has remained fairly stable in the past fifty years and may even have increased a little. This demographic stagnation reflects a balance among factors of erosion, including low fertility, population aging, and assimilation among one segment of American Jewry, and the growing share of the Orthodox due to higher fertility, an increase over time in the (initially quite low) proportion of children of mixed parentage who are identified and raised as Jews (chiefly due to more marital exogamy among Jewish women, the main predictor of the religious identity of children of intermarriage), greater willingness to self-identify as Jews in America's multicultural and individualistic climate, and large-scale immigration of Jews, mainly from the former Soviet Union and Israel (DellaPergola 2013a).

The numerical size of American Jewry is unquestionably the main issue on which demographers who concern themselves with this population disagree. This dispute has three different but complementary aspects. The first aspect is one of scientific methodology, i.e., the appropriate way to sample a rare population such as Jews. The answer may be a countrywide survey that enumerates people who have some present or past connection with Judaism, using an inclusive set of definitions of belonging. Or one may gather local Jewish surveys and merge them to yield an overall national estimate. Still others may rely on general surveys, each including a small number of Jewish respondents, conducted at different times, using different methods, and with partial coverage of the targeted population, adding them together to form a large enough sample of self-defined Jews, with the addition of estimates of the number of persons who defined themselves Jewish in terms other than religion and children. While some devotees of the first approach are critical of each of the other two methods, it does not work the other way around, i.e., the strength of the countrywide surveys is affirmed by a broad consensus.

Accordingly, it comes as no surprise that when the results of the Pew survey of the American Jewish population of 2013 were released, they were broadly accepted. The survey found 5.7 million Jews in the United States—4.7 million adults (82.5 percent) and 1.0 million children (17.5 percent). Among the adults, eight of ten were Jews by religion; the others defined themselves Jewish but with no religion.[4] In 2013, however, an additional million people reported no religious affiliation and defined themselves "partly Jewish," boosting the "Jewish population" to 6.7 million. Some of these partial Jews grew up as Jews or had two Jewish parents; most had one Jewish and one non-Jewish parent. Therefore different researchers adopt different numbers to argue for (i.e., similarity) or against (dissimilarity) the other approaches, those elicited by community or meta-analysis that correspond to the Pew 2013 findings. Expressed differently, "one survey for all, with everybody happy with their newly found proof that they were right" (DellaPergola 2014b:33).

This leads to a second controversial element in gauging the size of American Jewry, namely, who is a Jew? Traditionally, surveys considered as Jews only those who unequivocally defined themselves as such—either by religion or, among those who profess no religion, reporting themselves Jewish. Obviously, under circumstances of pluralism and the multicultural context that typify contemporary America, a dual group identity, be it racial, ethnic, national, religious, or ambivalence, is possible if not commonplace. Furthermore, a large majority of the partial Jews (eight out of ten) profess pride in being Jewish (DellaPergola 2014b). This in itself strongly reinforces the claim that such people are more Jewish than they are members of any other group. Conversely, only 4 percent of the partly Jewish stated that it is very important for them to be Jewish (leaving open the possibility that many others also find it important, but less so). Notably, the proportion among Jews with no religion who deem it very important to be Jewish is 20 percent. Generally speaking, among the various indicators, the religioethnic identification of partial Jews is weaker than that of Jews by religion or Jews without religion (DellaPergola 2014b). Even though partial Jews are definitely a fringe group in the Jewish population, they have some level of Jewish awareness. Bear in mind that NJPS 2000/01 included as Jews those individuals of Jewish background who did not define themselves as Jews and professed another faith, provided it was not antithetical to Judaism, i.e., not monotheistic.

The partial Jews put paid to the dichotomy of Jews and non-Jews (DellaPergola 2014b) by falling in between. Given their background, their eschewing of any other religion, and their identificational markers, they are closer to Jews than to non-Jews. At the present writing, with the Pew 2013 data not yet available, one can only suggest that this group should be treated differently from those who define themselves exclusively as Jews. A loose group identity should be judged through the lens of religious identification of attitudes and behaviors. When someone says he or she has a Jewish background, is proud to be Jewish, maintains important Jewish practices, and takes part in Jewish community activities, she or he should be included in the Jewish community for the purpose of estimating the community's size. Some partial Jews may even have stronger Jewish identification than some counterparts who profess Jewishness, but with no religion. Other partial Jews, who have a weak to nil Jewish background, display no particularistic Jewish interest, and partake of no Jewish activities, should be considered distant adjuncts of the core Jewish population and outliers from the Jewish collective, in a neutral zone but unaffiliated with any other religion.[5] Were such an approach applied, American Jewry would number somewhere between the low estimate (5.7 million) and the high one (6.7 million).

Painstaking assessment of partial Jews' affiliation is essential for the additional reason that American Jews are not discussed in a vacuum. Rather, they are often presented within the broad context of world Jewry. This introduces the third aspect of controversy among demographers who take an interest in the Jews: comparing the number of American Jews with that of their counterparts in Israel, more generally the number of Diaspora Jews versus those in Israel and the demographic patterns of each population group. It involves insights about the Jews' status as a minority versus majority in their country of residence, self-confidence contrasted with alienation, group vitality as against assimilation, and the environment that can best assure Jewish survival and hence valuable meanings. Size also matters for the distribution of Jewish public resources and the planning of educational and social services. In this regard, non-Jews by local official definitions who nevertheless have some connection with Judaism exist in other countries as well. The most representative group of this kind is that composed of former Soviet Union (FSU) immigrants who settled in Israel under the Law of Return but do not qualify as Jews under rabbinical law and, accordingly, are defined in Israel not as Jews but as "lacking religion." Many of them might have chosen to convert to Judaism, if this process in Israel, governed by Orthodox requirements, were easier. Still, their decision to immigrate to and live in Israel puts them through a "sociological conversion" (Cohen 2006). If social scientists include all partial Jews in the United States in the Jewish population, they should do the same for the FSU immigrants in Israel with no religion, augmenting Israel's Jewish population by half a million people. In fact, if only partial Jews in the United States who practice some form of Judaism were counted as American Jews, the "lacking religion" in Israel should also be included in that country's Jewish population. Paradoxically, these American partial Jews cannot immigrate to Israel if they lack a Jewish parent or are currently not married to a Jew. It is illogical to consider them Jews while those of no religion in Israel, who have some kind of Jewish kinship relationship, would not be counted in the Jewish population. The other extreme among the possibilities, if one were to maintain maximum uniformity among communities in defining "who is a Jew," would be neither to count the partial Jews in America nor any of the FSU immigrants of no religion in Israel as Jewish.

Either way, Jews are a small group in the American religious scene. Just the same, the religious composition of America sustains Will Herberg's description of the country as one of three large faiths: Protestant, Catholic, and Jewish (figure 1.1). Slightly more than half—51.7 percent—of adult Americans are Protestant, including 26.6 percent evangelical, 18.2 percent mainline, and 7.0 percent black; nearly one-fourth—24.1 percent—Catholic, and 2 percent Jewish. Another 1.7 percent define themselves as Mormons. The remainder either belongs to small Christian denominations (1.6 percent), other faiths including Buddhism and Hinduism (2.5 percent), Islam (0.4 percent), or no religion (15.9 percent).[6] Accordingly, even though the absolute number of Jews has not fallen in the past five decades, the dramatic growth of the American population at large has reduced the share of Jews by one-third, from 3.2 percent in the 1957 Current Population Survey to 2.0 percent in 2007, or to 2.2 percent if partial Jews are taken into account.

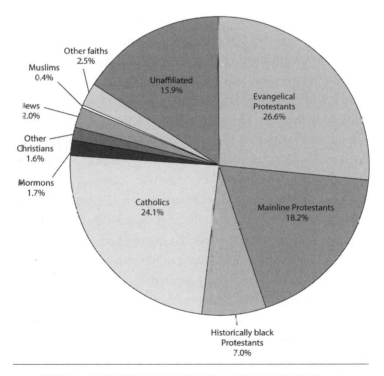

FIGURE 1.1. RELIGIOUS IDENTITY OF U.S. ADULT POPULATION, 2007

FERTILITY AND
INTERNATIONAL MIGRATION

Fertility is central to changes in the size of a population. The average number of children born to a woman, irrespective of her marital status, determines intergenerational replacement, i.e., a new generation's ability to quantitatively replace its predecessor. Religion figures importantly in fertility; religious requirements rooted in beliefs about marriage, family, and children share responsibility for demographic differences among members of different religious groups.

The ability to assess fertility patterns is somewhat limited because the Pew survey asked respondents whether they are parents or guardians of children under age eighteen who live at home, and how many such children there are in their household. This, however, does not attest to the total number of children that the respondent ever had; thus it prevents the possibility of calculating the average number of children per woman or of cohort fertility of women at an age group that more or less overlaps the end of their reproduction. Nevertheless, by comparing the average number of children below eighteen born to a Jewish woman in the Pew survey with the findings of the 2000/01 NJPS, which inquired into the total number of children born irrespective of their age, new estimates of American Jewish fertility can be proposed. Likewise, Jews' fertility patterns can be compared with those of Americans who profess other faiths.

As table 1.1 shows, an American Jewish woman has on average one child by age thirty and 1.7 by age thirty-five. If the data were comprehensive and covered all children, and not only those under age eighteen, women in the subsequent age cohorts would have more children; the fact that they have fewer suggests that some of the children have crossed this age threshold. Presumably, this happens mainly in religious and ultra-Orthodox households where marriage takes place at an early age, allowing these women to have grown-up children by their late thirties.

It is possible to adjust, albeit somewhat roughly, for the total number of children born to Jewish women by their late thirties and early forties by consulting information from the 2000/01 NJPS. The average number of children in each of the first three age cohorts is 35–45 percent higher in the Pew survey than in NJPS. The differentials between the surveys narrow in the next cohort, thirty-five to thirty-nine (13.2 percent). In the oldest cohort (forty to forty-four), they reverse direction, attesting to an increase in the number of children above age eighteen. Taking the smallest difference between the two surveys, the one in the thirty-five to thirty-nine age cohort, and applying it to the number of children in the oldest cohort of the NJPS, I obtain an average of 2.1 children per Jewish woman in the forty to forty-four cohort. One can, of course, apply to the eldest cohort of the NJPS not the differences between the surveys for the thirty-five to thirty-nine group but rather, for example, the mean differential among all the first four cohorts; this would yield an even higher level of fertility. Overall, the Pew survey seems to suggest higher levels of fertility than NJPS among younger women, possibly leading to higher completed fertility in subsequent years. No less important, Jewish women's completed fertility verges on, or stands only slightly below, the intergenerational replacement rate.[7]

The comparison of Jews with members of other religious groups in the Pew survey also suffers from a bias that may have been caused by differences in age at marriage and age at birth giving, both of which determine the mother's age when children reach age eighteen. What is clear is that Jews procreate later in life than Americans in most other religious groups. Thus, by age twenty-four, the average Jewish woman has 0.20 children as against almost half a child among other Americans (table 1.1). The difference narrows as age rises: in the thirty to thirty-four bracket it falls to 0.10. The religious groups that begin to have children especially early in life are evangelical Protestants, black Protestants, and Muslims. They are also the groups that attain very high fertility levels by age thirty to thirty-four, a time when, presumably, all their children are under age eighteen. These findings coincide with those of studies on the demography of American Christians, according to which evangelical Protestants and black Protestants have high fertility rates whereas those of mainline Protestants and Catholics are lower (Hunter 1983; Roof and McKinney 1987). Fertility at this stage is highest among Mormon women, at nearly three children on average. Jewish women of this age, in contrast, have one of the lowest fertility rates of all and a fortiori among the monotheistic religious groups (Christians, Muslims, Jews). This stands out even more in the next age cohort (thirty-five to thirty-nine).[8]

Another factor that is responsible for changes in a group's size and composition is international migration. It is true that any survey (or census) shows only one side of this phenomenon, in-migration, and says nothing about out-migrants. All the same, the U.S. largely attracts new population and repels few. The data in figure 1.2 show that one American Jew in ten was born abroad and that most of the immigrants reached the U.S. in the past three decades, mainly from the former Soviet Union, Israel, and

TABLE I.I CHILDREN BELOW EIGHTEEN BORN
AND PRESENT IN THE HOUSEHOLD, BY AGE OF
JEWISH WOMEN AND WOMEN OF OTHER
RELIGIOUS GROUPS, UNITED STATES, 2007

	Age				
Religious group	18–24	25–29	30–34	35–39	40–45
Jews [A]	0.20	1.09	1.71	1.59	1.37
(Jews, NJPS 2000/01) [B]	(0.13)	(0.59)	(1.04)	(1.38)	(1.86)
Differential (A–B)/A*100	35.0%	45.9%	39.2%	13.2%	-35.7%
Total other religions	0.44	1.33	1.83	1.80	1.38
Evangelical Protestants	0.50	1.56	2.02	1.87	1.30
Mainline Protestants	0.36	1.25	1.68	1.79	1.27
Historically black Protestants	0.49	1.59	2.00	1.76	1.30
Catholics	0.43	1.28	1.86	1.93	1.56
Mormons	0.39	1.56	2.95	2.75	2.31
Other Christians	0.36	1.01	1.81	1.74	1.08
Muslims	0.48	0.41	2.09	2.80	3.05
Other faiths	0.20	0.84	0.89	1.47	1.03
Unaffiliated	0.44	1.11	1.47	1.36	1.31

Iran. This rate strongly resembles the 12 percent average among the rest of the American population.

There are differences, sometimes substantial, among religious groups. Very few Protestants and Mormons (around 5 percent) are foreign-born. One-fourth of Catholics are foreign-born, mainly due to large-scale Hispanic immigration. The same rate recurs among other Christians and affiliates of other faiths (which include non-monotheistic religions), many of the immigrants coming from the Far East. Muslims have the highest rate

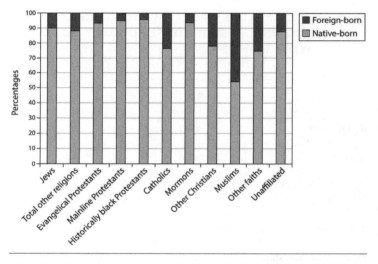

FIGURE 1.2. NATIVITY STATUS OF JEWS AND OTHER RELIGIOUS GROUPS IN
THE UNITED STATES, 2007

of foreign-born, nearly half bórn outside the United States. The
rate of foreign-born among the unaffiliated closely approximates
the national average.

Admittedly, the data used in this study were not classified
by years of arrival. Some immigrants may have arrived many
years ago and others more recently. Given what is known about
American immigration policy (specifically the 1965 Immigration
and Nationality Act) and the official immigration data, it can be
suggested that most of the immigrants arrived in the past four
decades and particularly since the mid-1980s.[9] Accordingly, from
the standpoint of international migration as a trigger of faster
population increase, Jews have a slight advantage over the Protestant majority, but a perceptible disadvantage relative to other
religious minority groups.

RELIGIOUS SWITCHING

Most people adhere to the faith into which they were born (Crockett and Voas 2006); accordingly, the higher the fertility of group members, the greater its numerical increase. Others, however, switch their religious identity by free choice, mostly adopting the faith of their spouse (Hout 2003). Retention or switching of religion reflects cost-and-benefit considerations in the open American market of spiritual goods and services (Kosmin and Keysar 2006; Roof 1993). According to cultural theory, religious preference is influenced by demographic and socioeconomic characteristics, and the most common pattern of religious switching is associated with upward mobility (Roof and McKinney 1987; Sherkat and Wilson 1995). Some individuals, however, waive religious identity altogether and adopt a nonreligious secular identity instead (Stark 1999). Recently, more and more religious switching in the U.S. mirrors social phenomena, foremost among middle-aged people of the "seekers" generation (Roof 1993). Notably, certain faiths attach "strings" to joining (or leaving). The interest of this study, however, is primarily sociological and not theological, hence, it concerns individuals' self-definition of their religious identity and changes in it, formal or not, between childhood and present.

The findings of the 2007 Pew survey suggest that roughly one American in ten (8.4 percent) who was raised as a Jew now had a different religious identity (without taking account of those who profess no religious affiliation [figure 1.3]; see also Smith 2009). The corresponding rate among other Americans is 13.5 percent. In other words, Jews are less inclined than gentile Americans to out-convert. A detailed investigation by main religious groups shows that Protestants have the lowest rate of switching from religion

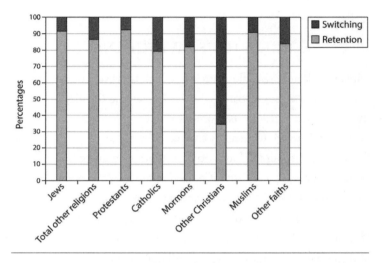

FIGURE 1.3. RELIGIOUS RETENTION AND SWITCHING AMONG JEWS AND
OTHER RELIGIOUS GROUPS IN THE UNITED STATES

of upbringing (although they probably do switch from one Protestant denomination to another). At the other end, those raised in other Christian faiths are the most inclined to switch religions (mainly to Protestantism). The religious group that most resembles the Jews in its rate of switching is the Muslims.[10]

The switching rate, of course, increases when those unaffiliated today are taken into account (table 1.2, upper part). About one-fourth of persons raised as Jews now define themselves as belonging to another religion or to no religion. The rate is slightly lower among those raised as Protestants (one-fifth) and higher among those brought up Catholic (one-third). In fact, among people raised in one of the large religious groups (Protestants, Catholics, Mormons, Jews, Muslims) and no longer identifying with their original faith, the strongest preference is nonaffiliation, at 13–16 percent among all groups. A large proportion of those raised in other Christian faiths (three-fourths) have a new religious preference today, three in ten having become Protestants and another one in four unaffiliated. Among those raised unaffiliated, more than half have adopted a faith of some kind, mostly Protestant.

Among Jewish out-converts only (table 1.2, middle part), some two-thirds became unaffiliated, 15 percent became Protestant, and 12 percent switched to one of America's smaller religions. Like Jews, about two-thirds of Muslims and Protestants who switched became unaffiliated. Most Muslims who chose a different religious identity, however, became Protestant. Protestants who switched religions, for their part, preferred Catholicism over other alternatives. Most persons who were raised as Catholics or Mormons and now have a different preference adopted a defined religion, most becoming Protestant. About half of those raised in other Christian denominations now define themselves as Protestants; another one-third are unaffiliated. Eight of ten who were raised with no religious affiliation and now have one define themselves as Protestants. Notably, the highest rate of switching to Judaism is found among those raised in other faiths: 3.5 percent.

Overall, for Jews, the effect of intergroup movements was a net loss of slightly more than 10 percent of the Jewish population in 2007 (table 1.2, lower part), or about half a million people. Notably, the entire loss is to the unaffiliated. Data not shown here, which narrow the calculation for religious groups alone (i.e., not taking into account those who became unaffiliated), suggest that the populations of out-converts and in-converts are similar in size, but that the latter hold a slight advantage, creating a net gain for Jewry of half a percent of its current population size. Protestants, Catholics, Mormons, and other Christians lost adherents. Jews had the third largest loss, following Catholics and other Christians. By contrast, Islam gained adherents, one-fifth

Religion of upbringing	Current religion, 2007									Distribution by religion of upbringing
	Protestants	Catholics	Mormons	Other Christians	Jews	Muslims	Other faiths	Unaffiliated	Total	
Percent distribution of religious upbringing										
Protestants	80.31	3.51	0.43	0.88	0.16	0.19	1.69	12.86	100.0	53.22
Catholics	14.91	68.02	0.39	0.90	0.14	0.06	1.54	14.02	100.0	31.71
Mormons	11.76	2.26	70.76	0.45	0.32	0.06	0.91	13.78	100.0	1.77
Other Christians	36.09	4.53	0.24	26.20	0.60	0.52	7.39	24.45	100.0	2.86
Jews	3.76	0.60	0.18	0.71	76.29	0.30	2.80	15.43	100.0	1.92
Muslims	6.86	0	0	0	0	76.47	0.98	15.69	100.0	0.35
Other faiths	9.88	1.98	0.53	0	1.05	0	69.17	17.39	100.0	0.87
Unaffiliated	39.21	6.52	1.16	1.38	1.21	0.47	3.39	46.63	100.0	7.30
Total	51.28	23.86	1.67	3.17	1.72	0.44	0.96	16.91	100.0	100.0

(continued)

(continued)

Percent distribution of religious switching

Religion of upbringing	Protestants	Catholics	Mormons	Other Christians	Jews	Muslims	Other faiths	Unaffiliated	Total	Distribution by religion of upbringing
Protestants	–	17.41	2.00	4.36	0.78	0.94	8.37	66.14	100.0	37.52
Catholics	46.00	–	1.21	2.80	0.44	0.18	4.76	44.64	100.0	35.90
Mormons	39.61	6.56	–	1.57	1.09	0.22	3.08	47.92	100.0	1.83
Other Christians	48.88	6.14	0.37	–	0.82	0.71	10.00	33.11	100.0	9.13
Jews	15.71	2.49	0.75	3.01	–	1.25	11.70	65.09	100.0	1.61
Muslims	29.17	0	0	0	0	–	4.17	66.66	100.0	0.29
Other faiths	32.05	6.41	1.71	0	3.42	0	–	56.41	100.0	1.16
Unaffiliated	79.61	13.24	2.36	2.81	2.46	0.95	6.89	–	100.0	12.56
Total	32.17	9.10	1.54	6.93	0.90	0.61	2.11	46.63	100.0	100.0

Net gain or loss as percent of current population

| | –2.94 | –31.75 | –4.95 | –75.79 | –11.54 | +20.93 | +65.50 | +56.96 | | |

of Muslims today having been raised in another faith or in no religion. The major gainers from religious switching are the other faiths and unaffiliated groups, at two-thirds and slightly more than half their current members, respectively.

AGE COMPOSITION

Demographic patterns of birthrates and life expectancy, on the one hand, and of migration and religious switching, on the other hand, are not evenly dispersed across the population, resulting in a different age structure for each religious group. Composition by age also reflects long-term effects of processes in earlier periods, such as the American baby boom from the end of World War II to the mid-1960s (Bouvier and De Vita 1991). Indeed, the age composition of the adult American Jewish population shows a salient bulge in the forty-five to sixty-four age cohort, which accommodates more than one-third of adult Jews (table 1.3). Their years of birth, 1943–1962, overlap the baby boom almost perfectly. The other age cohorts, though not of a similar range, weight about one-fifth of the population apiece. It is known, as indicated in the foregoing discussion of population size (section 2), that about one-fifth of American Jews are children. This slightly narrows the shares of the other age cohorts and, in particular, shows that the demographic basis of American Jewry—the zero to seventeen age cohort—is similar to if not slightly larger than the two cohorts following it. Still, the largest cohort is aged forty-five to sixty-four.[11] People in this cohort are expected to reach the top of the age pyramid in the foreseeable future, triggering faster population aging and eventually a surplus of deaths over births, i.e., negative natural increase.

The aging of the Jewish population is also documented by changes in age composition over the past fifty years. According to the 1957 Current Population Survey (U.S. Census Bureau 1958), 43 percent of adult Jews belonged to the eighteen to forty-four age group as against 42 percent in the 2007 Pew survey. A similar proportion in both surveys (37–38 percent) belonged to the middle-age (forty-five to sixty-four group), and 14 percent and slightly over 20 percent, respectively, populated the oldest cohort of sixty-five and above.

The age profile of Jews by religion differs from that of ethnic Jews in several ways. Jews by religion are older, as evidenced in the larger share of the two oldest age groups among them than among ethnic Jews. Among ethnic Jews, in turn, the higher share of the young (eighteen to twenty-nine) stands out. Overall, while among Jews by religion the split between the young (eighteen to forty-four) and the middle-aged and elderly (forty-five and over) is 40 percent versus 60 percent, among their ethnic Jewish counterparts it is quite even. This suggests that young people are not overly concerned about their ethnoreligious identity. It remains moot, however, whether this equanimity is a characteristic of age; if it is, once they move into the next age bracket, which is likely to involve marriage and child-rearing, they will become more group-conscious and identify as Jews by religion (or non-Jewish, in keeping with their spouse's religion). Alternatively, it may be a periodic characteristic that will accompany these young people in their mature years as well (given that they are largely the children of intermarriages, which are less likely to provide them with identification-strengthening inputs). A hint that it may be only a passing phenomenon is found in the split between Jews by religion and ethnic Jews in each age group and particularly between the two youngest age groups. Thus a vertical calculation of the data (not presented here) shows that while about one-fifth of the young are ethnic Jews and four-fifths are Jews by religion, the parsing in the next age group is 13 percent and 87 percent, respectively, and it stays there in the next age cohorts as well.

Interestingly, among adults, Jews are overrepresented in the eighteen to twenty-nine age bracket relative to the American population at large (table 1.3). At the other extreme of the age composition, the share of the elderly (sixty-five plus) is also greater among Jews than among non-Jews. The most conspicuous difference between Jews and the population at large is in the rate of those aged thirty to forty-four—20.4 percent and 29.4 percent, respectively. People who were thirty to forty-four years old in 2007 were born between 1963 and 1977 (the so-called Generation X). One may surmise that at this time, the end of the baby boom, the Jews' birthrate slowed more quickly and precipitously than that of other religious groups (DellaPergola 1980). Jews experienced accelerated educational and economic mobility and social integration during those years and gave higher priority to general social considerations than family matters. At that time, too, rising proportions of Jews married non-Jews, and some of their offspring were raised and identified not as Jews but as members of the non-Jewish parent's faith (usually Christian). Concurrently, since 1965, when U.S. immigration law was revamped, large numbers of migrants, who are typically young, have entered the country. Many immigrants in recent years are Hispanic and self-identify as Catholics; accordingly, they definitely contribute to the high proportion of those aged thirty to forty-four among this religious group. Overall, the dissimilarity index of age composition between Jews and non-Jews is 9.0.

A detailed look at the data suggests that mainline Protestants have the oldest age composition and Muslims have the youngest. Mormons, black Protestants, and affiliates of other faiths are also

TABLE 1.3 AGE COMPOSITION OF JEWISH AND
MAJOR RELIGIOUS POPULATIONS IN THE
UNITED STATES, 2007 (PERCENTAGES)

	Total	18–29	30–44	45–64	65+	Index of dissimilarity
Total Jews	100.0	21.2	20.4	36.7	21.7	–
Jews by Religion	100.0	20.0	20.7	37.3	22.0	–
Ethnic Jews	100.0	28.2	19.0	33.1	19.8	8.1
Total other religions	100.0	19.9	29.4	34.3	16.4	9.0
Evangelicals Protestants	100.0	16.6	29.0	35.8	18.6	8.6
Mainline Protestants	100.0	13.6	25.7	37.9	22.7	7.5
Black Protestants	100.0	24.2	26.2	34.3	15.3	8.8
Catholics	100.0	18.4	31.5	33.9	16.2	11.1
Mormons	100.0	24.3	32.5	28.2	15.0	15.2
Other Christians	100.0	19.1	27.5	36.4	17.0	7.1
Muslims	100.0	33.1	38.1	25.7	3.1	29.6
Other faiths	100.0	24.4	33.1	34.4	8.1	15.9
Unaffiliated	100.0	30.9	31.4	29.2	8.4	20.8

The index of dissimilarity reflects differences between total Jews and the specific religious group. For ethnic Jews, the index shows differences vis-à-vis Jews by religion.

typically quite young. Judged by the index of dissimilarity, the Jews most closely resemble the other Christians group (index = 7.1), mainline Protestants (7.5), evangelical Protestants (8.6), and black Protestants (8.8). By and large, then, Jews most closely resemble Protestant groups. The dissimilarity indexes are higher vis-à-vis Catholics (11.1) and Mormons (15.2). The largest difference between Jews and any individual religious group is with Muslims (index = nearly 30). As with the population at large, the most conspicuous differences between Jews and each of the other religious groups occur in the share of the thirty to forty-four age cohort, which is much lower among the Jews.

The past fifty years have seen stability, if not modest growth, in the number of Jews in the United States. This is a result of an internal dynamic of demographic factors that cancel each other out. They include a fertility rate that verges on intergenerational replacement, although, as other studies have suggested, "effective" Jewish fertility, i.e., children born to Jewish women who are also defined as Jews, is even lower (by about half a child); population aging due to the massing of large numbers of "baby boomers" in late middle age, not yet having attained a critical stage of more deaths than births; a relatively stable rate of foreign-born due to the continuation, albeit limited, of immigration (and, overall, a positive international migration balance); and equal numbers of out-converts and in-converts (but with significant switching to the unaffiliated). The Jews' demographic patterns are much different from those of Americans at large: lower fertility, a smaller share of foreign-born, a larger out-flux of adherents, and an older age composition. These patterns are more conspicuous than those of other religious groups at certain times and less conspicuous at other times. Further, the differences between Jews and one religious group may head in one direction and those between Jews and some other religious groups may turn the other way. The Jews' demographic stability, however, is overshadowed by an increase in the American population at large, meaning that the Jews' share in this population has declined. Nevertheless, more recently (since 1990), this trend seems to have reached a plateau.

2

SPATIAL AND SOCIOECONOMIC STRATIFICATION

THE RELIGION-CLASS NEXUS

RELIGIOUS AFFILIATION may correspond to structural characteristics of geographical and class niches (Demerath 1965; Dynes 1955; Niebuhr 1929; Roof and McKinney 1987; Reimer 2007; Smith and Fairs 2005). Religious allegiance shapes people's behaviors in various spheres including the social and economic. Indeed, most religious denominations have a disproportionate concentration of people who resemble one another in their educational attainment and income (Christiano, Swatos, and Kivisto 2008). This overlap derives, among other things, from distinct patterns of socialization as well as organizational and institutional involvement among members of religious groups. In fact, people who associate themselves with social classes adopt different beliefs for the purpose of adjusting them to socioeconomic success or failure and their special needs ("Class Model"; Marx 1978; Weber 1946). Insofar as religious minorities face discrimination, the aim of such discrimination at times is to deny them upward mobility; under such circumstances, religious categories overlap with social divisions that are rooted in a surfeit or deficit of rights (Pyle 2006).

Similarly, religions are differentiated in worldviews, including work ethics that may be significant to socioeconomic outcomes ("Cultural Model"; Durkheim 1995 [1912]; see also Berger 1967; Mack, Murphy, and Yellin 1956; Mayer and Sharp 1962). Religious affiliation affects perceived costs and perceived returns of decisions that people make in the course of their lives resulting in specific social and economic outcomes (Lehrer 2004). Different religions attribute different degrees of importance to the acquisition of social credentials and behaviors such as formal education, economic activities, political involvement, and family patterns (Lensky 1961). Within each denomination, these outlooks may be gender-differentiated with social and psychological gains that their religious institutions allocate to those who choose to stay home with their children (Lehrer 1995). The religion-class nexus also reflects groups' specific social and political interests, including minority standing and associated feelings of marginality and insecurity (Chua and Rubenfeld 2014; Park 1928). Likewise, a religious tradition is an independent factor that affects the individual's choice of where to live (Sigalow, Shain, and Bergey 2012). Religious-class relations are facilitated by economic inequality in the society at large, whereas denominational subcultures "embrace distinct theologies, styles of worship, and participation norms that have differential appeal to those of high or low social station" (Pyle 2006:67; see also Ryan 1981).

It is possible, however, that the broadening of religious and ethnic openness in the United States in the second half of the twentieth century, coupled with the relaxation of religious stringencies, has rendered these relations fluid and created more opportunities for upward social mobility and, accordingly, change in the class foundations of religion (Schwadel 2014; Wuthnow 1988). Modernization and the progress of society toward universalism mean the eradication of social organization mechanisms based on religious or ethnic belonging and the blurring of class boundaries among religious groups (Goldscheider and Zuckerman 1984; Turner 1993). This includes, among other things, the diminishing importance of ascribed affinities for social stratification (Erikson and Goldthorpe 1992). Likewise, nationwide economic growth reinforces universal criteria for occupational allocation that cross ethnic-class lines, allowing dominant and minority groups to have more similar economic opportunities (Goldscheider and Zuckerman 1984; Turner 1993). Moreover, today working-class people, chiefly those at the top of that class, have enough income to adopt lifestyles of a greatly expanded middle class (Christiano, Swatos, and Kivisto 2008).

Religious switching since the 1970s, which included a major increase in the proportion of the unaffiliated, and the restructuring of America's cultural mainstream with the falling share of mainline Protestantism and the growth of formerly small churches, helped to blur status boundaries among religious groups. Furthermore, large numbers of immigrants are redrawing the profiles of some religious groups, such as, for example, the impact of Hispanic immigrants on the socioeconomic profile of American Catholics. Advanced technology and improved access to knowledge are providing opportunities for greater socioeconomic homogeneity (Park and Reimer 2002; Pyle 2006).

This chapter examines three main social dimensions of American Jews: geographic patterns, level of education, and income. These affinities are assessed in comparison with other religious groups in the country. The analysis develops in such a way that each dimension is examined, along with other indicators, in the context of the dimension preceding it: level of education by geography, and income by geography and education. The description of relations between religious affiliation and levels of education and income is accompanied by investigation of the determinants of each of these dimensions, i.e., a multivariate analysis.

GEOGRAPHY AND
SPATIAL DISPERSION

American Jewry is typically identified with settlement in the northeast region of the country. At the tail end of their mass emigration from Eastern Europe in the early 1920s, two-thirds of American Jews lived in this region while only one in ten dwelled in the West and the South combined (Goldstein 1982). Amid changes in their occupational structure away from self-employment, mainly in trade, to wage employment in large corporations, nearly total academicization, and relaxation of rigid religious behaviors, ever growing numbers of Jews began to move to the Sunbelt regions in search of new economic opportunities, lifestyles, and climate (Goldstein and Goldstein 1996). There they gradually developed ethnic and religious infrastructures and services and made Judaism into a national American religion. Accordingly, the Jewish nature of an area may be a reason for as well as the result of migration. The importance of general environmental factors, on the one hand, and particularistic communal factors, on the other hand, varies over time and by stages in the personal life cycle (Rebhun 1997a; Rebhun and Goldstein 2006).

According to the official four-region partitioning of the United States, the largest Jewish concentration today is in the

Northeast, where nearly 42 percent of the Jewish population lives (about half of them, according to data not presented here, in New York State), followed by the Midwest at 11 percent (with an especially large concentration in Illinois), whereas each of the Sunbelt regions has a rather similar proportion of around one-fourth in the South (including slightly over one-third in Florida) and 22 percent in the West (three-fourths of whom in California); (table 2.1). This geographic dispersion is significantly different from their residential preferences in the middle of the twentieth century when the concentration in the Northeast was more salient (69 percent) and the presence in the South and the West was more scanty—8 percent and 11 percent, respectively; only the Midwest retained its share among the Jewish population (14 percent in 1957 and 11 percent in 2007).

There are differences in the geographic dispersion of Jews according to the way in which they are connected to Judaism. While a similar proportion of Jews by religion and Jews by ethnicity live in the Northeast, the former display a stronger preference for the Midwest and the South while an especially large proportion of ethnic Jews reside in the West. The evidence according to which many marginal Jews are drawn to the West suggests that either this region is attractive to this kind of Jew or that the conditions in this region attenuate awareness of ethnoreligious identity.

Jews' geographic dispersion is markedly different from that of Americans at large. Among the latter, only 18 percent live in the Northeast, namely less than half the share among the Jewish population. By contrast, the proportion that resides in the Midwest is twice that among Jews. Non-Jews also display a stronger preference than Jews for the South. Only the West accommodates a similar share of each population group, the Jewish and the non-Jewish. In the past fifty years, however, chiefly due to the growing share of the West and the South in the Jewish population, the differences in spatial dispersion between Jews and Americans at large have narrowed vigorously—from an index of dissimilarity (based on four regions) of 42.9 in 1957 to only 23.7 in 2007.

Of all the religious groups examined, the Jews have the highest concentration in the Northeast. Concurrently, most other groups prefer the Midwest and the South more strongly than Jews do. Of particular salience is the large proportion of evangelical and black Protestants in the South. These two groups are less inclined to live in the West. More than three-fourths of Mormons live in the West (mostly in Utah). Overall, judging by the index of dissimilarity, the three groups whose geographic dispersion most closely resembles that of Jews are Catholics (13.2), Muslims (19.3), and other Christians (19.5); the least similar groups are Mormons (54.3) and black Protestants (42.8). Besides the level of the index of dissimilarity, the differences between Jews and each religious group are unique and reflect historical, social, and religious circumstances of spatial preferences.

Another aspect of geographic dispersion is the division between urban and rural residence. Although the main distinction between urban and rural localities is size (Davis 1965), both spatial units reflect specific patterns of systematic links versus local solidarity and a sense of community, and the latter type also includes ideologies that promote the preservation of fundamental national values (Brown and Kandel 2006). Over time, however, the relation between familial and socioeconomic characteristics and geographic location has weakened (Albrecht 1998). With the decline in agriculture, the economic activities of rural inhabitants and their urban counterparts have largely converged (Castle 1998). Although these processes are asymmetric—urban

TABLE 2.1 REGIONAL DISTRIBUTION, JEWISH AND
MAJOR RELIGIOUS POPULATIONS IN THE UNITED STATES,
2007 (PERCENTAGES)

	Total	Northeast	Midwest	South	West	Dissimilarity index
Total Jews	100.0	41.6	11.4	24.9	22.0	—
Jews by religion	100.0	41.3	12.0	25.9	20.8	—
Ethnic Jews	100.0	43.9	8.0	19.1	29.0	—
Total other religions	100.0	18.3	23.7	36.4	21.6	23.7
Evangelical Protestants	100.0	9.6	23.3	50.4	16.7	37.4
Mainline Protestants	100.0	19.3	28.9	33.8	18.0	26.4
Black Protestants	100.0	12.9	19.4	59.7	8.0	42.8
Catholics	100.0	28.9	23.9	24.5	22.8	13.2
Mormons	100.0	4.3	7.1	12.5	76.1	54.3
Other Christians	100.0	21.7	19.8	28.7	29.8	19.5
Muslim	100.0	26.6	24.3	31.3	17.8	19.3
Other faiths	100.0	21.6	17.0	26.2	35.2	20.5
Unaffiliated	100.0	18.5	23.2	29.5	28.8	23.2

The dissimilarity index reflects differences between total Jews and the specific religious group.

impacts on rural areas surmount impacts in the other direction
(Lichter and Brown 2011), urban people are also adopting rural
values and styles (Woods 2009). The differences have narrowed
even more in recently established rural areas that are close to big
cities but outside the adjacent urban development, i.e., exurbs
(Lichter and Brown 2011). In fact, not all rural dwellers are
attached to the countryside socioeconomically; many commute
to town for work and by so doing maintain urban and rural orientations simultaneously (Brown et al. 1997).

Traditionally, American Jews have preferred to live in urban areas and particularly large metropolitan cities. This concentration is evidently associated with their high educational and occupational qualifications and their affinity for employment opportunities and lifestyles that are obtainable mainly in an urban or metropolitan environment. In these areas, large numbers of Jews have participated in the intensive suburbanization of the American urban middle class.

Evidence from the mid-twentieth century shows that only 4 percent of American Jews lived in rural areas, as against more than one-third of Americans at large (U.S. Census Bureau 1958). By 2007 the proportion of rural Jews dropped to 2.9 percent, but that of non-Jews retreated even faster to 18.8 percent (table 2.2). Slightly more than half the Jews live in suburbs, and four of every ten Jews reside in a city center. Among Americans at large, too, more live in suburbs than in cities—one-half and one-third, respectively.

Notably, Jews' residential patterns vary by type of Jewish identity. Jews by religion are more concentrated in suburbs than ethnic Jews, who exhibit a stronger preference for the city. An important explanation for these differences is marital status, in which 57.5 percent of ethnic Jews were unmarried at the time of the survey as against 43.1 percent of Jews by religion. Even among the married, however, slightly more ethnic Jews than Jews by religion preferred a rural locality over city life, whereas the share of each group living in the suburbs was very similar.

Muslims resemble Jews in their relative disinclination to live in rural localities. However, they entertain a stronger preference for the city and a weaker one for the suburbs than Jews. Black Protestants are also more concentrated in cities than in suburbs.

TABLE 2.2 JEWISH AND MAJOR RELIGIOUS POPULA-
TIONS IN THE UNITED STATES BY TYPE OF COMMU-
NITY, 2007 (PERCENTAGES)

	Total	Urban	Suburban	Rural
Total Jews	100.0	42.2	55.0	2.9
Jews by religion	100.0	41.3	56.4	2.3
Ethnic Jews	100.0	47.1	46.7	6.1
Total other religions	100.0	32.0	49.2	18.8
Evangelical Protestants	100.0	24.8	48.3	27.0
Mainline Protestants	100.0	26.1	51.5	22.4
Black Protestants	100.0	49.8	37.3	12.9
Catholics	100.0	34.7	54.1	11.2
Mormons	100.0	32.5	48.7	18.8
Other Christians	100.0	36.5	51.0	12.5
Muslims	100.0	53.1	44.3	2.6
Other faiths	100.0	38.8	49.3	11.9
Unaffiliated	100.0	36.4	46.3	17.3

All other religious groups have a higher share of members in suburban areas than in urban ones.

EDUCATIONAL ATTAINMENT

Jews' social mobility is facilitated by the fact that achieved, rather
than ascribed, characteristics are paramount determinants of
an individual's status in contemporary American society. The
recognition of education as a preeminent social value has also

furthered the Jews' successful integration into general society (Goldstein 1992). A positive attitude toward learning also corresponds to Jewish tradition, which values not only religious studies but secular knowledge as well (Hartman and Hartman 1996). Perhaps more than any other American religious or ethnic group, Jews have very impressively utilized their civil liberties and opportunities to position themselves on the upper rungs of the educational ladder (Lipset and Raab 1995). This is reflected in evidence to the effect that Jews, as a group, have the highest level of schooling in the U.S. (Pyle 2006) and are one of the most educated populations in world history (Kosmin and Lachman 1993).

The Jews' educational attainments were already evident by the middle of the twentieth century. At that time, Jews boasted more than twice the share of college graduates than the American population at large—17 percent and 8 percent, respectively (Goldstein 1969). The gap widened in subsequent years; by 2007, 57 percent of Jews aged twenty-five years old and over held academic degrees as against only slightly over one-fourth of their American counterparts at large (figure 2.1). Although both the Jewish and the non-Jewish American populations improved their levels of education, the change was more rapid among the former; accordingly, the dissimilarly between the two population groups widened from 14 in 1957 to 30 in 2007. Notably, data not presented here indicate substantial differences among Jews according to type of group affiliation: Jews by religion are more educated than ethnic Jews, with 59 percent of the former having academic education as against 43 percent of the latter. Some of the difference is probably associated with the younger age composition of ethnic Jews.

Not only are Jews better educated than non-Jews; their educational profile surpasses that of all other religious groups (figure 2.1). The differences vis-à-vis the other groups are wide: as far

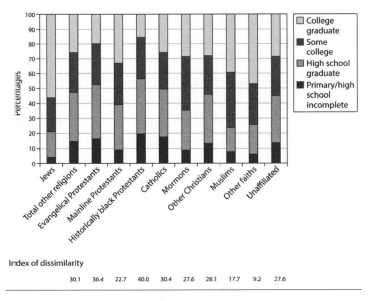

Index of dissimilarity

| 30.1 | 36.4 | 22.7 | 40.0 | 30.4 | 27.6 | 28.1 | 17.7 | 9.2 | 27.6 |

FIGURE 2.1. EDUCATIONAL ATTAINMENT OF JEWS AND OTHER
RELIGIOUS GROUPS IN THE UNITED STATES, 2007

as academic education is concerned, they range from 9 percent relative to those affiliated with other faiths to 40 percent relative to Evangelical Protestants. At the bottom of the education scale, the share of Jews who fail to complete high school is the lowest among the religious groups. The strongest similarity is between Jews and people affiliated with other faiths with an index of dissimilarity of 9.2, followed by Muslims, with an index of dissimilarity of 17.7. The Jews are most different from black Protestants and evangelical Protestants.

Within each religious group there are differences in education by main demographic characteristics (table 2.3). Such a detailed look yields a more refined comparison among the groups, one parsed within distinct demographic categories. Among the Jews, the young (eighteen to twenty-nine) exhibit the lowest share of persons with academic education, presumably because many have not yet completed their studies. They are followed by the oldest age group. The share of those with academic education rises inversely to age until the highest rate, three-fourths, is attained by the thirty to forty-four cohort, attesting to the ongoing academicization among American Jews. This is also largely true for other religious groups. Indeed, the share of degree holders among young people is quite similar across all religious groups; nevertheless, in older age groups Jews are much different from counterparts in other religions. The relatively small differences between Jews and Muslims and adherents of other faiths recur by age cohorts.[1] The educational attainments of Jewish men and women resemble each other. Gender similarity in education is typical of the American population at large and of most religious groups. The main exception is the Mormons, among whom the percentage of men with college degrees is much larger than that among women (one-third and one-fourth, respectively). Hence intergroup differences in education are similar among men and women. Interestingly, among adherents of other faiths, more women than men have academic education.

Different regions in the United States may appeal to people who have specific characteristics, including education. This reflects the uneven dispersion of economic activities in fields that require academic schooling and, in turn, occupational credentials. In this context, it bears noting that, in strong correspondence with level of education, slightly more than half of American Jews practice professional occupations (among them, 12 percent of men and 6 percent of women are doctors, lawyers, or college-level teachers), and another 15 percent in each of the gender groups hold managerial positions (Chiswick 2007). The share of college-degree holders among Jews in all four regions is rather similar, with slightly more representation in the Northeast and the West. This pattern, of strong concentration of academically educated persons in the two regions at the extremes of the continent and weaker concentration in the two mid-continental regions, is also typical of evangelical Protestants, other Christians, and the unaffiliated. Mainline Protestants who have college degrees tend to live in the South and the West in higher concentrations; highly educated Muslims congregate in the Northeast and the South. Thus the differences among religious groups vary considerably by regions of residence.

Foreign-born Jews are less educated than Jews born in the U.S. Accordingly, immigrants lower the Jews' average level of education. Differences of this type, but even larger, are found among Catholics. In contrast, immigrants who are mainline Protestant, Muslim, other Christian, affiliates of other faiths, and unaffiliated are better educated than their American-born counterparts. This is particularly salient among Muslims: in this group immigrants are three times as likely to have academic schooling as the American-born are. Muslim immigration to the United States is exceptionally positive-selective; this helps to explain the relatively small differences between Jews and Muslims in educational attainment. Insofar as education influences the residential environment, the workplace, and cultural preferences, the educational attainments of Jews and Muslims in the U.S. create opportunities for strong interaction between them, with the possibility of broader implications for Jewish-Arab relations in the U.S. and elsewhere, including the Middle East.

INCOME LEVELS

Another important dimension of stratification is income. Income, more than occupation (a parameter that does not take working

TABLE 2.3 EDUCATIONAL ATTAINMENT (PERCENT COLLEGE GRADUATE) BY MAJOR SOCIODEMOGRAPHIC CHARACTERISTICS AMONG JEWS AND OTHER RELIGIOUS GROUPS IN THE UNITED STATES, 2007

	Jews	Total other religions	Evangelical Protestants	Mainline Protestants	Black Protestants	Catholics	Mormons	Other Christians	Muslims	Other faiths	Unaffiliated
Age											
18–29	18.5	16.5	16.3	18.4	13.1	18.2	19.0	14.6	21.4	17.4	16.4
30–44	74.6	33.0	25.9	41.9	21.0	32.4	38.4	28.5	51.4	51.9	40.6
45–64	71.9	29.0	20.9	37.8	16.1	28.1	29.6	34.5	43.9	61.0	33.9
65+	51.6	19.0	11.2	25.7	10.1	17.1	19.8	29.2	58.3	52.0	9.1
Gender											
Male	56.9	26.7	20.1	35.4	14.8	26.4	32.7	31.6	40.0	43.2	28.0
Female	55.3	25.5	19.6	31.8	16.5	25.5	25.4	25.4	39.5	51.8	29.3
Region of Residence											
Northeast	58.2	29.0	21.8	30.7	14.4	28.4	29.0	33.2	49.5	51.2	33.3
Midwest	55.9	23.7	18.3	29.1	13.8	26.0	28.8	22.8	25.5	47.1	22.3

(continued)

(*continued*)

	Jews	Total other religions	Evangelical Protestants	Mainline Protestants	Black Protestants	Catholics	Mormons	Other Christians	Muslims	Other faiths	Unaffiliated
South	51.5	24.3	18.9	36.7	16.2	26.0	27.0	26.3	46.3	43.6	24.5
West	57.5	29.3	23.6	37.3	20.2	22.4	28.8	29.8	30.4	46.9	34.7
Nativity Status											
Native-born	56.6	26.2	19.8	33.2	15.9	29.1	28.5	24.9	20.2	41.2	27.8
Foreign-born	52.2	25.1	19.9	38.2	14.0	14.6	29.9	39.2	62.2	64.2	34.3

conditions into account), attests to the extent to which human capital is economically rewarded. Accordingly, income appropriately reflects a minority's economic success in overcoming the devalued status associated with ascribed traits of religious status and ethnicity. Income underscores employers' recognition of individuals' credentials that may differ by specific group belonging, among other things.[2] In an attempt to track Jews' income over time (1957 to 2007), and changes in the differences between them and non-Jews, four categories of annual income in 1957 are distinguished: up to $3,999 ("low"), $4,000–$6,999 ("middle"), $7,000–$9,999 ("high"), and $10,000 and over ("very high"). Given the increase in U.S. dollar purchasing power in the interceding five decades, more than seven times over (7.4; Consumer Price Index), the corresponding income categories for 2007, are up to $30,000, $30,000–$49,000, $50,000–$99,000, and $100,000+.

In 1957, the income distribution of Jewish households already surpassed that of American households at large.[3] Only 22 percent of Jewish households were in the low income bracket as against 35 percent of American households. In the "very high" bracket, the rates were 25 percent and 8 percent, respectively. The index of dissimilarity between the groups was .22. By 2007, both populations had experienced a decline in the share of low-income households (to 13 percent among Jews and 31 percent in the population at large), whereas the proportion of very-high-income households climbed (to 46 percent of Jewish households and 17 percent of American households). Also, the share of the middle-income group contracted considerably among Jewish households (from 33 percent in 1957 to 12 percent in 2007) and more moderately among non-Jewish American households (from 38 percent to 22 percent, respectively) Accordingly, the index of dissimilarity between the two populations widened to 29.

Jews have the highest income of any American religious group (figure 2.2). The share of low-income Jews is half, if not less, of the corresponding rate among every other religious group. At the opposite extreme, the share of very-high-income households is at least twice as large among Jews as among counterparts in other religious groups. When all four income levels are taken into account, the group most similar to the Jews, although notably smaller in its income, is other faiths, an aggregate that includes many people of Indian and Chinese origin, with an index of dissimilarity of 22. A somewhat similar level of dissimilarity was found between Jews and mainline Protestants (25) and with Catholics and the unaffiliated (27). The largest differences were between Jews and black Protestants (47).

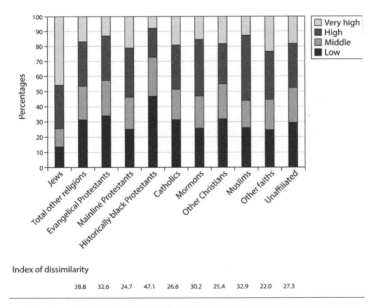

FIGURE 2.2. FAMILY INCOME OF JEWS AND OTHER RELIGIOUS GROUPS IN
THE UNITED STATES, 2007

TABLE 2.4 INCOME LEVEL (PERCENT "VERY HIGH") BY MAJOR SOCIODEMOGRAPHIC CHARAC-
TERISTICS AMONG JEWS AND OTHER RELIGIOUS GROUPS IN THE UNITED STATES, 2007

	Jews	Total other religions	Evangelical Protestants	Mainline Protestants	Black Protestants	Catholics	Mormons	Other Christians	Muslims	Other faiths	Unaffiliated
Age											
18-29	36.6	12.4	10.8	15.8	7.3	14.1	9.4	11.7	0	13.6	12.7
30-44	57.5	19.6	15.4	24.2	9.9	21.1	16.8	23.3	20.0	26.1	21.9
45-64	53.5	20.8	15.7	26.6	9.2	23.7	21.5	22.1	8.7	30.4	22.0
65+	28.5	8.1	5.6	9.7	4.0	8.6	12.6	9.9	25.0	14.5	11.3
Gender											
Male	50.8	19.5	15.5	24.3	11.0	21.7	17.8	24.7	9.6	24.4	19.8
Female	39.7	14.6	13.2	18.2	6.4	16.8	13.8	13.6	17.1	23.1	16.7
Region of Residence											
Northeast	50.3	18.8	11.7	19.1	8.2	22.6	13.2	19.4	7.5	21.8	19.1
Midwest	34.0	14.6	11.2	16.6	9.1	17.7	17.6	15.4	11.4	27.5	13.4
South	43.3	15.7	12.7	23.6	7.7	18.2	20.6	16.7	14.7	20.2	17.0
West	45.9	20.3	18.3	25.3	10.1	17.2	14.7	21.7	19.4	25.9	24.0

(continued)

Nativity Status

Native-born	46.3	17.1	13.1	20.8	8.3	21.5	15.9	17.4	8.8	20.2	17.9
Foreign-born	41.4	16.2	13.8	25.7	7.1	11.9	10.8	22.8	16.9	34.3	23.7

Education

Primary/HS incomplete	9.5	4.4	4.0	4.7	3.4	3.7	11.0	9.8	0	6.2	5.6
HS graduate	31.2	9.4	8.0	10.0	4.3	10.9	9.2	10.9	10.9	13.4	10.9
Some college	32.4	14.4	14.3	14.4	7.0	17.4	13.9	13.1	0	7.7	15.6
College graduate	57.0	35.2	27.6	40.0	24.5	39.5	25.1	36.6	26.1	39.2	34.8

Household income levels vary with respondents' age in the form of a reverse U curve: the proportion of people who have high income is low in youth, rises and peaks at age thirty to sixty-four, and then falls back (table 2.4). This probably reflects various rewards for labor associated with experience, being retired (among the elderly), and marital status, i.e., number of breadwinners, which is smaller among the young and the elderly due to the prevalence of singles and the widowed in the respective groups. The differences between the thirty to forty-four and forty-five to sixty-four age groups in the shares of very-high-income persons are often small. In view of these consistent patterns, Jews have an advantage over affiliates of other faiths in all age cohorts. The largest differences between Jews and non-Jews were found among the youngest age cohort and the oldest age cohort (a rate of very high-income persons that is three times greater than among total non-Jews) and narrows slightly, albeit remaining more than twice as large, in the two middle-aged cohorts. Another characteristic observed among most groups, with the exception of Muslims, is that men report higher income than women do. Since this is household income, it is likely affected by gender differences in income among the unmarried and the widowed. A detailed look reveals large gender differences among black Protestants as opposed to below-average differences for evangelical Protestants, members of other faiths, and the unaffiliated.

The income of Jews in the Northeast surpass those of their peers who live in other regions of the country. The spatial differences are small between Jews in the Northeast and those in the West, but very substantial relative to Jews in the Midwest. Among non-Jews, too, the proportion of very-high-income persons is high in the Northeast and the West, to the slight advantage of the latter region. The ranking of regions varies among religious groups. Within this disuniformity, the West stands out for the highest proportion of people reporting very high income in six of the eight religious groups (evangelical, mainline, and black Protestants; other Christians; Muslims; and the unaffiliated). Only Catholics resemble the Jews in having the largest concentration of very high income in the Northeast. Among Catholics in all three other regions, however, the proportion of people at the highest income level is very similar. These variations by geography suggest that the income advantage of Jews may exceed the average countrywide advantage in some regions and fall short of it in others. In the Northeast, for example, the difference between Jews and evangelical Protestants is greater than for the United States at large; at the same time, in the West, and particularly in the Midwest, the Jews' advantage in the share of people with very high income over those of other faiths is smaller than among total non-Jews.

The same religious groups in which the native-born have higher rates of college education than the foreign-born are also those in which the native-born out-earn the foreign-born and vice versa. The former include Jews, black Protestants, Catholics, and Mormons; the latter constitute, primarily, mainline Protestants, other Christians, Muslims, other faiths, and the unaffiliated. The differences between the American-born and the foreign-born are especially large among Muslims (twice as much) and for affiliates of other faiths.

Not surprisingly, income is positively associated with education. As the education level ascends, so does the proportion of people with very high income. Even when education levels are similar, Jews out-earn non-Jews. However, as education rises the differences between Jews and each of the other religious groups narrow. This diminishing of differences is especially salient among mainline Protestants, Catholics, and persons of other faiths. Among those who have college degrees, the remaining differences between Jews and non-Jews are probably related to the degree attained—bachelor's, master's, doctorate, professional specializations such as law or medicine, and also, perhaps, the academic institution attended, especially if they are elite colleges or universities that can affect wage levels.

DETERMINANTS OF SOCIOECONOMIC ATTAINMENT

The foregoing discussion revealed differences among religious groups in major social and economic characteristics. These characteristics, however, do not operate independently. Rather, they are often interrelated, reflecting, at least partly, the effect of one characteristic on the other. A more refined and probing investigation, namely a multivariate analysis, considers all the sociodemographic variables jointly and evaluates the net effect of each sociodemographic variable on educational attainment and income while holding all the others equal.

The explanatory sociodemographic variables in this study include age, gender, marital status, region of residence, community of residence, and nativity status (and, for income, level of education as well). For each of the variables of education and income, four models were run: model 1 for Jews, model 2 for non-Jews, model 3 for the total population with Jews as against non-Jews as one of the explanatory variables, and model 4 for the entire population as well, decomposing non-Jews according to their specific religious affiliation. The power of each model for explaining variations of the variable that stands at the center of the analyses (i.e., the dependent variables of education and income) was calculated.[4]

Determinants of Education

American Jews of middle age are more likely to have higher education than those in the oldest group (sixty-five plus; model 1, table 2.5). Unsurprisingly, the young are at an educational disadvantage because some have not yet completed postsecondary studies. Being widowed is negatively associated with education. The findings suggest that geography is an important determinant of education: Jews who live in the South are less educated than the reference category of Jews in the Northeast, as are those who dwell in suburbs or rural localities in comparison to their urban peers. Foreign-born Jews are less educated than American-born ones. Overall, the sociodemographic variables explain nearly 19 percent of the differences in American Jews' levels of schooling.

Among non-Jews (model 2), all age cohorts under age sixty-five have significant higher levels of education than those in the oldest cohort (sixty-five plus). Women have significantly higher levels of education than men. Those who live alone, be it due to being single, having divorced, or having become widowed, are likely to have less education than those who are married. People who live in the two farthest-removed regions of the American continent, the Northeast and West, have an education advantage over those in the Midwest and the South. Further in the geographic context, whether as a result or as a cause, rural residence is associated with lower levels of formal education. Being born outside the United States deters schooling relative to the American-born. Overall, the directions of the relations between sociodemographic characteristics and education are highly similar among Jews and non-Jews, and in the few cases where they head in different directions (e.g., gender or living in a suburb) they are statistically insignificant for one of the population groups. Among non-Jews, however, the sociodemographic variables explain only about 8 percent of the variation in education—less than half the explanatory power of a similar model for Jews.

When group affiliation is incorporated into the model (model 3), a positive relation is found between being Jewish and higher education. A Jew is 1.2 times more likely to be one rung higher on the educational ladder (on a four-level scale: high-school dropout, high-school graduate, some college, college graduate) than a non-Jew, all other variables in the model held constant. The relation remains rather stable when non-Jews are decomposed into specific religious groups (model 4) and their relation with education was evaluated relative to that of mainline Protestants (the reference group).[5]

This detailed analysis shows that Jews have an education advantage over all other religious groups (i.e., they have the highest positive coefficient). They are followed by Muslims and affiliates of other faiths. All other religious groups have an education disadvantage relative to mainline Protestants. Within this hierarchy, black Protestants are the least likely among American religion denominations to advance educationally (i.e., the highest negative coefficient). Notably, the disaggregation of non-Jews by specific religious groups slightly increased the ability of the model to explain variance in educational attainment—from about 9 percent in the third model to 11 percent in the fourth.

TABLE 2.5 EFFECTS OF SOCIODEMOGRAPHIC CHARACTERISTICS AND GROUP AFFILIATION ON EDUCATIONAL ATTAINMENT, UNITED STATES 2007

	Jews	Non-Jews	Total with group belonging	Total with religious identity
Age 18–29	-1.080***	0.200***	0.174***	0.181***
Age 30–44	0.879***	0.715***	0.712***	0.733***
Age 45–64	0.862***	0.548***	0.551***	0.564***
Female	-0.154	0.079***	0.078***	0.094***
Single	-0.118	-0.234***	-0.236***	-0.223***
Divorced/ separated	-0.249	-0.395***	-0.395***	-0.394***
Widowed	-0.760***	-0.686***	-0.691***	-0.685***
Midwest	0.035	-0.110***	-0.109***	-0.087***
South	-0.273*	-0.242***	-0.242***	-0.155***
West	0.146	0.065***	0.066***	0.048*
Suburban	-0.289**	0.005	0.000	-0.019
Rural	-0.540	-0.563***	-0.564***	0.589***
Foreign-born	-0.492**	-0.904***	-0.893***	-0.935***
Jews	-	-	1.263***	0.914***
Evangelical Protestants	-	-	-	-0.606***
Black Protestants	-	-	-	-0.821***
Catholics	-	-	-	-0.475***
Mormons	-	-	-	-0.188***
Other Christians	-	-	-	-0.267***
Muslims	-	-	-	0.662***
Other faiths	-	-	-	0.616***
Unaffiliated	-	-	-	-0.297***
% variance explained (R^2)	18.9%	7.8%	3.8%	11.2%

* $p < .05$; ** $p < .01$; *** $p < .001$; a) the numbers are odds ratios from an ordinal logistic regression; b) the reference categories are as follows: age—65+; gender—male; marital status—married; region of residence—Northeast; community of residence—urban; nativity status—native-born; group belonging—non-Jews; religious identity—mainline Protestants.

Determinants of Income

Income is also determined—even more strongly than education—by sociodemographic characteristics and religious belonging (table 2.6). Among Jews (model 1), young age (especially thirty to sixty-four) is correlated positively with income. In contrast, being a woman, being unmarried (whether single, divorced, or widowed), living in the Midwest or the West, and living in rural localities are significant predictors of lower income. The strongest predictor of income is education, holders of academic degrees being three times as likely as high school dropouts (the reference group) to advance from one income level to the next.

Similar relations were found for non-Jews (model 2), with one main difference: living in the West raises, as opposed to decreases, the likelihood of having high income. It is possible that Jews who live in the West engage chiefly in high-tech wage labor, whereas most of their peers in the Northeast (the reference group) continue to practice traditional Jewish occupations in medicine, law, and business—foremost real estate—that are typified by a high proportion of self-employment and concentration at the top of the income ladder. Among non-Jews, the West opened up economic opportunities for large numbers of highly educated people who had advanced occupational credentials, leaving the less-advanced population behind in the Northeast.

The sociodemographic variables are more efficient in explaining income variation than they are in explaining differences in education attainment. It is possible that the explanatory power improved because of the incorporation of an independent variable, education, that relates strongly with income. Unlike education, for income the sociodemographic variables were more efficient in explaining variance among non-Jews than that among Jews: 34.9 percent and 23.8 percent, respectively.

Ceteris paribus, Jews have higher income than non-Jews—a 0.93 greater likelihood of being at a higher income level than the preceding one (model 3). They also have a stronger probability of higher income than mainline Protestants (the reference group) and, in fact, have an advantage over all other religious groups (model 4). As in the case of education, black Protestants are the group that has the lowest level of income relative to mainline Protestants. The Jews' sizable advantage over the other groups may stem from differences in the distribution of people with academic diplomas between the bachelor's and more advanced degrees, as well as specific occupations and particularly concentration in well-paying fields such as medicine, law, and business. Overall, the sociodemographic characteristics and religious affiliation explain nearly 36 percent of the variation in family income levels among Americans.

Over the past five decades, Jews and non-Jews alike have been experiencing accelerated geographic and socioeconomic mobility. These processes have reinforced the similarity between the two populations in spatial dispersion across the four official regions of the continental United States and away from rural localities to urban and suburban areas. The Jews have gained in both education and income and have done so more quickly than their non-Jewish counterparts, resulting in the widening of the gaps between the two populations. Notably, the empirical observations of the Jews' geographic preferences and educational and economic attainments are reaffirmed by the findings from the 2013 Pew Research Center Survey of U.S. Jews (Pew Research Center 2013), which were identical to those from 2007.[6] These socioeconomic

TABLE 2.6 EFFECTS OF SOCIODEMOGRAPHIC CHARACTERISTICS AND GROUP AFFILIATION ON INCOME, UNITED STATES, 2007

	Jews	Non-Jews	Total with group belonging	Total with religious identity
Age 18–29	0.191	0.424***	0.421***	0.452***
Age 30–44	0.749***	0.767***	0.765***	0.797***
Age 45–64	0.703***	0.931***	0.926***	0.953***
Female	-0.364***	-0.417***	-0.416***	-0.412***
Single	-0.321*	-0.930***	-0.917***	-0.887***
Divorced/ separated	-0.832***	-1.298***	-1.290***	-1.276***
Widowed	-0.838***	-1.369***	-1.360***	-1.352***
Midwest	-0.372*	-0.131***	-0.138***	-0.121***
South	-0.226	-0.094***	-0.100***	-0.021***
West	-0.303*	0.086***	0.076***	0.103***
Suburban	0.068	0.289***	0.282***	0.258***
Rural	-0.959**	-0.251***	-0.255***	-0.281***
Foreign-born	-0.225	-0.552***	-0.545***	-0.589***
High school graduate	1.494***	1.191***	1.192***	1.187***
Some college	2.093***	1.809***	1.809***	1.798***
College graduate	2.967***	2.871***	2.866***	2.831***
Jews	-	-	0.930***	0.761***
Evangelical Protestants	-	-	-	-0.290***
Black Protestants	-	-	-	-0.640***
Catholics	-	-	-	-0.083***
Mormons	-	-	-	-0.348***
Other Christians	-	-	-	-0.167**
Muslims	-	-	-	-0.305**
Other faiths	-	-	-	-0.168***
Unaffiliated	-	-	-	-0.181***
% variance explained (R^2)	23.8%	34.9%	35.3%	35.8%

*p < .05; **p < .01; ***p < .001; a) the numbers are odds ratios from an ordinal logistic regression; b) the reference categories are as follows: age—65+; gender—male; marital status—married; region of residence—Northeast; community of residence—urban; nativity status—native-born; education—not completed high school; group belonging—non-Jews; religious identity—mainline Protestants.

processes, corroborated by the spatial evidence, attest to the acceptance and success of Jews in American society. In fact, the Jews' faster upward mobility is solidifying their concentration on the high rungs of the social ladder and, in turn, may abet a degree of separatism on the part of this successful group. Irrespective of sociodemographic characteristics, the data show that Jews are more inclined than non-Jews to acquire higher education and are expected to have higher income. Looking at the three socioeconomic dimensions together and ranking the degrees of similarity between Jews and each of the other religious groups, one sees that Jews are most similar to mainline Protestants (especially in education and income, slightly less in geographic dispersion) to adherents of other faiths (consistently in all three dimensions, although not at the highest similarity level), Muslims (in geographic dispersion and education), Catholics (in geography and income), and other Christians (in geography and income). The groups farthest from the Jews are black Protestants and evangelical Protestants. Structural similarity or its opposite, distance, may have implications for intergroup relations and opportunities for social interaction and hence interfaith understanding.

3

INTERFAITH MARRIAGE

AMALGAMATION UNDER THE CANOPY

P EOPLE HAVE a natural inclination to maintain "primordial links" to their own ethnic, national, or religious group (Geertz 1963; McPherson, Smith-Lovin, and Cook 2001). In addition, historical conditions, political considerations, or theological constraints ("third party" influence; Sporlein, Schlueter, and van Tubergen 2014) may hinder conditions of equality and cooperation between members of different groups, thereby inhibiting interfaith social and familial ties (Connolly 2000; Jackman and Crane 1986). Some religions strongly restrict marriage with members of other religious groups or at least demand the maintenance of religious identity and firm religious commitment in such a union (Kelley 1972; Lehrer and Chiswick 1993). Moreover, religious groups differ in the centrality that they attach to the family, their emphasis on community, and the importance of social and residential segregation, all of which may affect spousal choices (Greeley 1977).

People may also be concerned about connections between family patterns (i.e., homogeneous versus heterogeneous marriages) and continuity or change in the group culture. The power of gathering inward and the scope of contacts and relations with other groups are central factors in determining the perpetuation or alteration of the cultural and ideological heritage, including religious and national habits or traditions (Sandomirsky and Wilson 1990). A high frequency of religiously heterogeneous family contacts may blur structural and cultural particularism and even bring about involvement—both symbolic and religious—in the rituals of other religious faiths. Given the centrality of the family in children's socialization, it is reasonable to assume that a homogeneous nuclear family will transmit a clear and well-defined feeling of group belonging (Kalmijn 2010; Xie and Goyette 1997), whereas a mixed family environment is likely to expose children to a variety of religious group values and orientations that are disconnected from a coherent ideological framework and fissured with internal contradictions (Goldstein 1992; Gordon 1964; Lieberson and Waters 1988).

For socioeconomically disadvantaged members of a minority group, however, marriage with a member of the majority society may leverage upward mobility and improve the standard of living (Goldscheider 2004). Thus, some people place economic considerations ahead of cultural or religious concerns in order to attain admittance to the local mainstream (O'Leary and Finnas 2002). Somewhat different considerations may operate in the case of upper-stratum members of the minority group, for whom high intermarriage rates may attest both to social integration and acceptance and to the importance accorded to personal autonomy in matters connected to romance and marriage (Alba and Nee 2003; Magid 2013). Notwithstanding, class theories predict a positive relationship between social achievements and endogamy among minority groups (Kalmijn 1993; Sporlein, Schlueter, and van Tubergen 2014). This is especially true among members of high-achieving ethnoreligious groups that, by striving to maintain socioeconomic structural uniformity, enhance the likelihood of intragroup marriage (Phillips and Fishman 2006; O'Leary and Finnas 2002).

Theological and social barriers associated with belonging to a religious group and differences in the importance that members of different faiths ascribe to group continuity suggest that, even after differences in individual socioeconomic characteristics are taken into account, the extent of interfaith marriage in general, and that involving adherents of specific religious backgrounds in particular, may not be evenly dispersed across religious groups. This chapter examines rates of intermarriage among Jews and other main American religious groups and asks which religious groups are the most and the least likely to marry one another. This is followed by an examination of the relations between sociodemographic indicators and marriage patterns. A multivariate analysis is used to assess the independent role of identifying with a particular religion on endogamy or exogamy. Because the RLS did not ask about marital history, the analysis is confined to current marriages.

LEVELS AND COMPOSITION OF INTERMARRIAGE

Until the middle of the twentieth century, intermarriage was rare among American Jews. That is, Jews attained their social and economic integration into American society without marital assimilation (amalgamation). Only around 4 percent of married Jews in 1957 had a spouse who had neither been born Jewish nor had converted to Judaism (a "prevalence measure"; Mueller and Lane 1972). By 1970, this rate had grown to roughly 7 percent. This average, however, masked very different patterns among marriage cohorts (an "incidence measure")—from 2 percent of those who married in the first quarter of that century to more than one-fifth among those who wed in the five years between 1965 and 1970 (Schmelz and DellaPergola 1983). Marital heterogeneity continued to increase in the next four decades, to nearly one-fourth (23.2 percent) of all Jews who got married in 2007—a sixfold percent upturn (figure 3.1). Notably, although this rate attests to the acceleration of intermarriage, it falls slightly short of the findings of NJPS 2000/01, which revealed that nearly one-third of married Jews had a non-Jewish partner. The differences between the two sources—the 2007 Pew survey and NJPS 2000/01—derive from the method of calculation. Thus Jews who have reported having religiously unaffiliated partners were not included among the intermarried in this study. Furthermore, the 2007 Pew sample was somewhat biased in the direction of Jews by religion as against ethnic Jews. Taking religiously unaffiliated spouses into account, one boosts the intermarriage rate to 32 percent of all married Jews.

Among American Protestants in 1957, slightly fewer than one in twenty (4.5 percent) were intermarried. Among Catholics, the rate was 12.1 percent (Mueller and Lane 1972). By 2007 the rate had more than tripled among Protestants (evangelical, mainline, black) to 13.9 percent and increased by around one-half among Catholics to 16.8 percent.[1] In other words, the tendency to amalgamation has grown stronger among all three large American religions, but it did so much faster among the Jews than among the others. A detailed look does reveal two groups that had higher intermarriage rates than the Jews: Other faiths and other

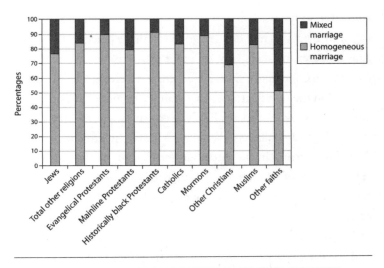

FIGURE 3.1. MARRIAGE COMPOSITION AMONG JEWS AND OTHER
RELIGIOUS GROUPS IN THE UNITED STATES, 2007

Christians. All other religious groups had lower rates of amalgamation than those of the Jews. Data not shown here attest to major differences between Jews by religion and ethnic Jews, with only one-fifth of the former and a hefty three-fourths of the latter married to a spouse of a different religion.

Intermarrying Jews have a clear preference for Catholic spouses, leaving Protestant ones far behind (table 3.1). Fifty years ago the opposite was the case, as more intermarried Jews had Protestant spouses than Catholic ones. This may be related to changes in the attitudes of the Catholic Church, which no longer objects to interfaith marriage (Rebhun 1999). Intermarried Protestants, of whatever denomination, mate chiefly with Catholics and vice versa, i.e., most intermarried Catholics have Protestant spouses. The second most-favored group among both Protestants and Catholics who intermarry is other Christians. Largely, then, Protestants and Catholics who intermarry do so with members of other Christian denominations. Similarly, other Christians involved in intermarriage usually have a Christian spouse, either Protestant or Catholic. Intermarried Mormons prefer Protestants and Catholics at a rather similar rate. Most American Muslims who choose to marry outside their faith do so with Protestants. Perhaps the greatest diversity in choice occurs among Americans of other faiths who marry Protestants and other Christians at similar rates of slightly under one-fifth and mate with Catholics at around 10 percent. Other Christians and adherents of other faiths have the highest rates of intermarriage with Jews—around 2 percent of all married persons in each group.

SOCIODEMOGRAPHIC CHARACTERISTICS OF INTERMARRIAGE

How do mixed marriages vary in their sociodemographic characteristics? Does marital amalgamation reflect different preferences of specific segments of the population by age, gender, geography, and socioeconomic status, or is it evenly distributed across the population? And do amalgamation and sociodemographic characteristics interrelate similarly or differently among Jews and non-Jews? Table 3.2 attempts to answers these questions. It shows that Jews have an especially high rate of intermarriage among those aged thirty to forty-four: one of every three Jews in this cohort has a non-Jewish spouse. This rate is twice as high as that among their eldest peers (sixty-five plus), attesting to a meaningful

TABLE 3.1 GROUP BELONGING BY SPOUSE'S RELIGIOUS IDENTITY AMONG MARRIED
PERSONS IN THE UNITED STATES, 2007 (PERCENTAGES)

Respondent's religious belonging	Spouse's religious identity							
	Jews	Protestants	Catholics	Mormons	Other Christians	Muslims	Other faiths	Total
Jews	76.8	6.9	13.7	0.1	1.8	0.1	0.6	100.0 (852)
Evangelical Protestants	0.2	89.7	7.3	0.5	2.2	0.1	0.1	100.0 (12,852)
Mainline Protestants	0.7	79.4	15.3	0.4	3.8	0.1	0.3	100.0 (8,316)
Black Protestants	0.6	91.0	5.1	0.2	2.8	0.3	0	100.0 (1,874)
Catholics	0.9	13.6	83.2	0.2	1.8	0.1	0.2	100.0 (11,461)

(continued)

(*continued*)

Mormons	0.3	5.1	4.1	88.8	0.8	0	0.9	100.0 (987)
Other Christians	2.3	15.6	12.9	0.1	68.9	0	0.1	100.0 (681)
Muslims	0	15.1	1.1	0	0	82.7	1.1	100.0 (185)
Other faiths	2.0	18.9	9.3	0.2	18.2	0.2	51.1	100.0 (883)

Numbers in parentheses are weighted absolute sample cases.

intergenerational trend. Indeed, the rate of intermarriage among those in the youngest cohort (eighteen to twenty-nine) is lower. Yet it is likely that Jews who marry so early in life have a strong religious orientation, meaning that this cohort is overweighted with religious Jews. If so, the differences between the two age cohorts (eighteen to twenty-nine and thirty to forty-four) should not be interpreted as a weakening of the tendency to intermarry among young Jews. Among non-Jews, too, the intermarriage rate is higher among the young than among the elderly. These changes, however, are not gradual; each of the three youngest age cohorts reports a very similar rate of religious exogamy. Religious groups that display similar patterns to those of the Jews, i.e., an increase in the tendency to intermarry in younger age groups, are evangelical, mainline, and black Protestants and also, to some extent, Catholics and other Christians. Other groups have different and unique patterns; the contrast between Muslims—among whom "marrying out" is closely related to youth—and adherents of other faiths, among whom the highest rates are found in the oldest cohorts, stands out in particular.

Intermarriage is more typical of Jewish men than of Jewish women. In this respect, Jews differ from other Americans among whom gender differences are negligible. In fact, gender similarity in mixed marriages is a characteristic shared by all non-Jewish American groups. The exceptions are Catholic women and other Christian women who have a stronger tendency to amalgamate than their male counterparts. The religious group most similar to the Jews, in which men have a significantly higher intermarriage rate than women, is the Muslims.

Jews in the two Sunbelt regions (South and West) have higher intermarriage rates than Jews in the Northeast and the Midwest. These patterns distinguish Jews from other Americans, among whom the highest intermarriage rates are found in the Northeast and the West and the lowest rates in the South. These latter patterns characterize the Protestant groups. In contrast, among Catholics, Mormons, and people of other faiths, very high rates of amalgamation are found among members in the Midwest. Again, the patterns most closely resembling the Jews are those of Muslims. However, Muslims evince very large differences between the West and the Northeast. In the other geographic dimension—type of locality—Jews and non-Jews also behave differently: the rate of intermarriage among Jews in agricultural and suburban localities is perceptibly higher than that among urban Jews, whereas among non-Jews the relation is inversed: a higher intermarriage rate in town than in the countryside. Jews are a rather uncommon sight in rural localities; accordingly, they may be there due to migration after having married a non-Jew. Rural life is more common among non-Jews; it therefore generates local intimacy and a strong sense of community that are likely to increase the probability of marriage with natives of the individuals' locality or nearby rural localities, hence within the same religious faith. Like Jews, for Catholics, Muslims, and adherents of other faiths, intermarriage rates are higher among inhabitants of rural localities than among urban counterparts.

American-born Jews are two and a half times more likely than foreign-born Jews to have non-Jewish spouses. The differences by nativity status are smaller among non-Jews. The proximity between native-born and foreign-born among the non-Jewish population is the result of very different patterns among Protestant denominations and among the Mormons. These two groups have a large surplus of mixed marriages among immigrants relative to the intermarriage rate of the American-born, contrasting with Catholics, other Christians, Muslims, and adherents of other faiths, among whom intermarriage is more typical of the American-born than of the foreign-born.

Amalgamation among Jews is not necessarily associated with high stratification. In fact, it appears to be exceptionally typical of those who do not share the Jews' socioeconomic success. The highest rates of intermarriage are observed among Jews who have some college education (presumably those who drop out in the middle) and those of middle income. In contrast, intermarried non-Jews stand out for their high social status; their proportion rises gradually in tandem with each of the education and income indicators. The exceptions are Muslims and adherents of other faiths, who resemble the Jews in having high rates of intermarriage among members who belong to the middle class in education and income. For each religious group separately, members whose characteristics resemble those of the majority marry within the group, whereas those who are different—disadvantaged in the Jews' case or advantaged among non-Jews—find their partners in other faith groups. This coincides with the view that structural similarity amplifies the identity of interests, lifestyles, and values, and, in turn, group cohesion, including marital endogamy. Accordingly, the Jews' unique social and economic attainments, which distinguish them from the rest of the American population, inhibit assimilation.

CAUSES OF INTERMARRIAGE

A finer examination of the determinants of marital exogamy versus endogamy may be provided by a multivariate analysis. Here, as in the previous chapter on social and economic attainments, four models are presented: Jews, non-Jews, the population at

TABLE 3.2 INTERMARRIAGE RATE BY MAJOR SOCIODEMOGRAPHIC CHARACTERISTICS AMONG JEWS AND OTHER RELIGIOUS GROUPS IN THE UNITED STATES, 2007 (PERCENT)

	Jews	Total other religions	Evangelical Protestants	Mainline Protestants	Black Protestants	Catholics	Mormons	Other Christians	Muslims	Other faiths
Age										
18–29	20.7	17.6	12.6	27.2	11.6	18.1	7.4	28.0	30.3	49.0
30–44	32.6	16.7	11.2	24.2	12.7	17.1	9.2	27.8	14.9	35.5
45–64	21.9	16.6	10.8	21.2	6.3	17.0	17.6	32.9	16.1	58.2
65+	16.2	10.7	5.7	11.1	5.0	13.9	8.5	35.1	0	67.1
Gender										
Male	26.7	15.4	10.0	20.4	8.9	15.6	11.3	29.4	19.7	48.8
Female	18.8	16.4	10.7	20.8	9.0	17.9	11.2	32.7	12.7	48.9
Region of residence										
Northeast	19.7	19.2	18.9	28.1	14.7	13.5	13.5	26.8	8.6	44.6
Midwest	19.6	17.8	11.3	19.7	14.9	20.4	27.8	35.1	7.4	60.7
South	29.0	11.8	7.0	13.8	5.8	19.4	14.5	27.6	14.5	44.7
West	26.6	18.7	15.0	28.5	17.6	14.1	9.4	36.2	57.1	49.5

(continued)

	Jews	Total other religions	Evangelical Protestants	Mainline Protestants	Black Protestants	Catholics	Mormons	Other Christians	Muslims	Other faiths
Community type										
Urban	19.3	15.9	11.8	20.5	9.6	15.0	9.1	27.4	18.3	43.8
Suburban	25.6	17.4	12.1	23.2	10.5	16.7	15.0	34.9	14.3	48.6
Rural	27.8	11.9	6.1	14.7	3.4	22.6	4.5	26.4	37.5	78.1
Nativity status										
Native-born	24.8	16.3	9.8	20.0	7.9	19.8	10.9	33.0	32.3	74.2
Foreign-born	10.6	13.3	18.3	22.3	24.6	7.6	16.7	26.0	9.2	16.9
Education										
Primary/HS incomplete	16.0	11.8	11.0	18.2	8.4	9.1	37.0	38.5	0	48.3

(*continued*)

(*continued*)

	Jews	Total other religions	Evangelical Protestants	Mainline Protestants	Black Protestants	Catholics	Mormons	Other Christians	Muslims	Other faiths
HS graduate	28.7	15.1	10.6	20.8	6.9	16.9	10.7	18.2	60.0	59.0
Some College	34.1	16.2	10.0	21.5	9.8	18.4	10.3	31.7	20.0	59.2
College graduate	20.3	18.0	9.9	20.2	11.2	19.6	8.6	40.0	9.8	43.2
Income										
Low	0	12.9	10.5	18.2	8.8	12.0	16.9	19.8	14.3	53.9
Medium	35.3	15.3	9.3	22.3	5.3	16.9	11.0	21.2	45.8	62.9
High	25.5	16.5	10.3	20.4	10.5	19.8	9.5	35.7	17.0	41.7
Very High	23.5	19.5	11.3	22.8	16.5	19.6	16.4	37.3	0	47.7

large, Jews as against non-Jews as an independent variable, and the population at large parsed by specific religious groups. The explanatory sociodemographic variables are age, gender, region of residence, type of locality, nativity status, and education. It should be noted that preliminary analyses that also introduced income in the left-hand column of the independent variables elicited a jumble of findings due to a strong correlation of this variable with education. Hence income is excluded from the models. The findings of the binary logistic regression should be read in such a way that a coefficient greater than 1 denotes a positive relation between the independent variable and the likelihood of intermarriage, whereas a coefficient below 1 indicates a negative relation.

Jews aged thirty to forty-four are more than three times as likely to have a non-Jewish spouse as elderly Jews (aged sixty-five plus; table 3.3). A positive and significant relation, albeit slightly weaker, was obtained for the forty-five to sixty-four cohort. As suggested earlier, the population of those who are both young (eighteen to twenty-nine) and already married evidently includes many religious Jews, making the relation with composition of marriage statistically insignificant. All other things being equal, the likelihood of marrying outside the faith is 40 percent lower among Jewish women than among Jewish men. Intermarriages are more characteristic of relatively new regions of Jewish settlement, i.e., the West and the South. Irrespective of region, marital exogamy is more prevalent among suburban Jews than among urban ones. Foreign-born Jews tend much less than American-born Jews to intermarry. Couples' religious composition is unaffected by social stratification (i.e., education). Notably, when the education variables were removed from the model and replaced with income levels, the resulting expectation was that Jews of lower income would be more intermarried than those of very high income. The descriptive findings and the analytic results of the multivariate analysis are in harmony, implying that acute socioeconomic stratification does not prompt but rather impedes Jewish amalgamation. Overall, the sociodemographic variables were successful in explaining 11.4 percent of the variance in marital composition, endogamous or exogamous.

Young non-Jews are also more likely than their older counterparts to marry out of the faith. Additional similarities between Jews and non-Jews are the positive relation between suburban living and intermarriage and the negative relation between being foreign-born and intermarriage (although the intensity of the relation is weaker among non-Jews in both cases). Concurrently, among non-Jews, living in the South inhibits intermarriage and living in the West has no significant relation with the religious composition of married couples. (For Jews, both regions encourage intermarriage.) Rural living weakens the likelihood of having a spouse of another faith, whereas among Jews the relation was insignificant. Perhaps the most conspicuous difference between the populations lies in the nexus of education and intermarriage: positive among non-Jews and insignificant among Jews. Furthermore, among the former, the intensity of these relations rises in tandem with increase in education, as evidenced by the size and significance of the coefficients. Interestingly, even though the number of sociodemographic variables that have statistically significant effects is greater among non-Jews than among Jews, these variables were able to explain only a little (3 percent) of the variance in couples' religious composition—one-fourth of the explanatory power of the same set of variables for Jews.

With the entire population taken together and all sociodemographic variables held constant, being Jewish diminishes the likelihood of marrying outside the faith by 30 percent relative to being a non-Jew (model 3). Jews are slightly more likely to intermarry than members of the reference group (mainline Protestants, model 4) but the differences are not statistically significant. A stronger tendency to intermarry than that of mainline Protestants is characteristic mainly of other Christians and adherents of other faiths (due to whom, evidently, Jews are less inclined to intermarry than the non-Jewish aggregate). Other religious groups—black Protestants, Catholics, Mormons, and evangelical Protestants—are less predisposed to intermarriage than mainline Protestants; this is probably associated with a more rigid religious doctrine among the former (Kalmijn 1998). The group that is most similar to the Jews in its tendency to intermarry is American Muslims. That black Protestants are among the least likely to intermarry may be associated with a racial aspect that, although having attenuated over the years, still plays a role in African Americans' marriage patterns (Qian and Lichter 2007; Romano 2003).

The decomposition of non-Jews into individual religious groups greatly enhanced the ability of the model to explain differences in marriage patterns. The explanatory power of model 4 is two and a half times higher than that of the preceding model, which draws a rough distinction between Jews and non-Jews. This emphasizes the importance of intragroup factors—theological, communal, or other at the environmental level—in understanding intermarriage in America, which seems to be more central than individual-level characteristics. This is particularly the case for non-Jews as against Jews, with the implications that this may have for aspects of individualism versus collectivism and group commitment.

Judging by trends in the extent of their intermarriage, Jews have undoubtedly effected a fine integration into American society. In

TABLE 3.3 DIRECTION (> 1 POSITIVE, < 1 NEGATIVE) AND MAGNITUDE OF THE EFFECTS OF SOCIODEMOGRAPHIC CHARACTERISTICS AND GROUP BELONGING ON INTERMARRIAGE, UNITED STATES, 2007

	Jews	Non-Jews	Total with group belonging	Total with religious identity
Age 18–29	1.606	1.836***	1.828***	2.026***
Age 30–44	3.373***	1.651***	1.674***	1.804***
Age 45–64	1.707*	1.636***	1.633***	1.674***
Female	0.609**	1.046	1.030	1.041
Midwest	1.255	0.948	0.967	1.045
South	1.649*	0.591***	0.616***	0.745***
West	1.921**	1.025	1.056	1.199***
Suburban	1.492*	1.096**	1.108**	1.147***
Rural	2.058	0.756***	0.760***	0.811***
Foreign-born	0.364**	0.696***	0.687***	0.480***
High school graduate	1.503	1.149*	1.152*	1.030
Some college	2.106	1.166**	1.179**	1.019
College graduate	0.879	1.296***	1.274***	0.965
Jews	-	-	0.701***	1.183
Evangelical Protestants	-	-	-	0.455***
Black Protestants	-	-	-	0.406***
Catholics	-	-	-	0.787***
Mormons	-	-	-	0.388***
Other Christians	-	-	-	1.893***
Muslims	-	-	-	1.093
Other faiths	-	-	-	4.446***
% variance explained (R^2)	11.4%	3.0%	3.0%	8.1%

* $p < .05$; ** $p < .01$; *** $p < .001$; a) the numbers are odds ratios from a binary logistic regression; b) the reference categories are as follows: age—65+; gender—male; region of residence—Northeast; community of residence—urban; nativity status—native-born; education—primary/high school incomplete; group belonging—non-Jews; religious identity—mainline Protestants.

the past fifty years their intermarriage rate has risen dramatically. This process is still continuing: the 2013 Pew survey found that four of every ten currently married Jews have a non-Jewish partner.[2] Admittedly, the tendency to intermarry is more a general than a Jewish phenomenon in contemporary America, but Jews are participating in it with unusual celerity. In this process, the preference among intermarrying Jews has shifted from a Protestant spouse to a Catholic one. The stronger religious devotion of Catholics has the potential to weaken the Jewish spouse's group identity more than Jewish-Protestant unions would, diminishing the vitality of American Jewry at large. Likewise, many mixed marriages involving Protestants and Catholics take place between these two broad denominations, which, despite some major differences between them, are both Christian. Implications similar to those of amalgamation involving Jews may exist among Muslims who choose spouses of another faith, mostly Protestantism, and among Americans of other faiths who marry Christians. Although intermarriages among most religious groups take place mainly with members of Christian denominations, the matrix that links the individual's religious identity with that of his or her spouse suggests that intermarriage in America connects people of almost all confessions with each other.

Intermarried Jews carry several sociodemographic markers. Jewish religious exogamy is related to younger age, male gender, residence in the American South and West, residence in suburban and rural areas, being American-born, and being of low social status. Young American-born non-Jews are also more likely to marry out of the faith than older ones are. In other characteristics, non-Jews and Jews intermarry differently: men and women prefer this marital pattern similarly; mixed marriage among non-Jews is associated with residence in the two farthest-removed regions (Northeast and West), and it is more common among urbanites and among the well-educated.

The tendency of Jews to intermarry is strongly encouraged by their social and economic affinities. If these factors are taken into account, i.e., in a hypothetical situation where Jews resemble non-Jews in key factors such as age, social status, and geographic dispersion, they would be less inclined than other Americans to marry outside their faith. This may provide evidence that, under individual circumstances typical of those of the general population, Jews would be more aware than non-Jews of their specific identity and have a stronger psychological sense of being different than others, resulting in the internalization of norms of endogamy (Kalmijn 1998). Jews would be especially less likely to "marry out" than other Christians and adherents of other Faiths. Still, they would be more likely to take this step than evangelical Protestants, black Protestants, Catholics, and Mormons, and as likely as Muslims. Overall, both socioeconomic indicators (structural explanations) and religious affiliation (cultural explanations) figure importantly in understanding marital amalgamation in the United States and in assessing this phenomenon among members of given religious groups through a comparative perspective of peers from other faiths.

Finally, it is important to note that mixed marriages per se have no effect on the size of the Jewish population. Mixed marriages may expand or diminish the Jewish population due to three accompanying factors: equilibrium of accession to and secession from Judaism, differences in fertility patterns among endogamous versus exogamous couples, and gain or loss due to the religious identity of the offspring of the mixed marriages. Each of these components has experienced significant transformation over time. The directions of the change have not always been that uniform, which created some confusion and disagreements that the fresh data from the 2013 Pew survey may resolve.

In 1970, the first NJPS revealed some 85,000 "Jews by choice," i.e., people who had not been born Jewish but identified as Jews at the time of the survey. Some of these new Jews had formally converted; others had simply adopted a Jewish self-identity. Conversely, an estimated 65,000 people who had been born Jewish did not identify themselves as such at the time of the survey. Thus the balance of conversion was in favor of the Jewish community, albeit a marginal one within the larger trend of Jewish population growth. Although they could not be examined systematically, it stands to reason that most of the intergroup transitions were the outcomes of marital unions between those born Jews and those who were not. By 1990, there were already 185,000 people who had not been born Jewish but identified themselves as Jews and 210,000 born Jews reporting having abandoned their Jewishness and adopted another faith. The accession-secession balance, positive in 1970, was negative by now, although still marginal relative to the total size of American Jewry (adopted from Massarik 1977; Kosmin et al. 1991). More recently, however, the cost to American Jewry of interfaith transitions has become meaningful. According to calculations from the Pew 2013 Jewish population survey, 160,000 persons who had not been born Jewish now define themselves as Jews as against 480,000 persons who had been raised as Jews (by religion) but now profess a different religious preference—a loss of 300,000 members of the Jewish population.[3]

American Jews' fertility rates are low, being on the border of intergenerational replacement and below those of the non-Jewish white population. In the past, the fertility rate of women in mixed marriages was about one-fourth lower than that of women in endogamous unions (DellaPergola and Schmelz 1989). By 2013, the disparity widened to more than one-third (1.8 versus 2.8, respectively; Pew 2013:40). The differences may be explained in three ways: exogamous couples marry later in life, they are better educated, and they are concerned that raising children and determining their religious identity might precipitate spousal conflict.

Indeed, one of the main aspects of the demographic implication of high rates of intermarriage is the religious identity of these marriages' offspring. An equal distribution by which half the children are defined as Jews and the other half according to the religions of the non-Jewish parent would not cause any loss to the Jewish population. The findings of NJPS 1990, however, show that only one-fourth of these children were raised as Jews; 45 percent were raised in a non-Jewish faith, and the remaining 30 percent were reported as growing up with no religious affiliation (Kosmin et al. 1991). In 2013, one-fifth of intermarried Jews reported that they were raising their children as Jews by religion, one-fourth as partly Jewish, 16 percent as Jews but not by religion or in any other form, and roughly one-third (37 percent) as not Jewish in any sense (Pew Research Center 2013:8–9). Since the definitions of partly Jewish and "other forms" are somewhat vague, it is hard to estimate accurately the proportion of offspring of intermarried parents who are raised as Jews. What seems more certain is that the tendency of intermarried couples to define their children as Jews has increased to somewhere between one-third and one-half. By implications, the fertility of intermarried Jews has recently caused little if any loss to the Jewish population.

Obviously, the religious affiliation of the offspring of mixed marriages, be it with Judaism or with a non-Jewish parent's confession, is ultimately determined by the offspring themselves when they reach adulthood. In this regard, for the first time, the 2013 Pew Survey documented the religion of adult children of intermarriage. The findings reveal an increase from older to younger generations in the proportion of those identifying as Jewish. While only one-quarter of Americans aged sixty-five and above with intermarried parents are Jewish today, 39 percent of their counterparts in the thirty to forty-nine age bracket currently profess a Jewish identity, and 59 percent of young adults (under age thirty) do so (Sasson 2013). Thus intermarriage is transmitting Jewish identity to a growing number of Americans (Smith and Cooperman 2013). That the propensity of children of intermarriage to identify as Jews is most salient among young adults has "skewed the overall Jewish population toward the young" (Sasson 2014), contributing to the potential of future demographic growth among American Jewry.

Overall, religious conversions due to intermarriage have taken a toll on the Jewish population. Intermarried Jews have fewer children than their endogamous counterparts. Children of intermarried parents are somewhat more likely to be raised Jewish or partly Jewish than in the faith of the non-Jewish parent. Over generations there is an increase in the proportion of adult children of intermarried parentage to identify as Jewish. The various aspects of intermarriage are acting in clashing directions in their effect on the number of Jews in the United States. The next chapter evaluates a complementary effect of intermarriage, namely, the cultural one, on the patterns and rhythm of Jewish identification.

4

RELIGIOUS IDENTIFICATION

THE MULTIFACETEDNESS
OF RELIGIOSITY

THE AMERICAN population is differentiated between Jews and non-Jews, and among the latter by specific groups, on the basis of religious identity, i.e., the individual's self-concept of group belonging and the value and emotional significance that she or he attaches to it (Beit-Hallahmi 1989; Galkina 1996; Herman 1977; London and Hirschfeld 1991; Tajfel 1981; Owens, Robinson, and Smith-Lovin 2010). This subjective identity is "carried out in terms of self-reported statements or placement in social categories" (Dashefsky and Shapiro 1976:5; see also Fearon 1999), as compared with objective or normative definitions guided by religious laws that dictate family affiliation or formal joining (Miller 1963). The identity of the individual is determined by the continual interplay between primordial, or ascribed, affinities and patterns absorbed from his or her proximate social environment (Herman 1977; Isaacs 1975) and is particularly used to make sense of how people share things with some while differing from others (Brubaker and Cooper 2000).

Individual identity refers to aspects that are meaningful for a person's group membership including his or her religious belonging (Deaux 2001). The manifestation of group consciousness or identity evolves amid the gradual merging of various identifications and behaviors of the individual (Erikson 1963, 1968). Thus, different self-definitions of group belonging or family background will reflect the nature of religioethnic commitment that is expected to be translated into beliefs, attitudes, values, rituals, and other distinct group behaviors (Hogg and Abrams 1988). This approach largely treats identity as an ideological phenomenon and assigns identification a more tangible, concrete meaning.[1]

Group identity may take on various forms (Levy 2009). Often it combines religious, ethnic, and cultural elements. Some of these elements are specific to each religious group, reflecting rituals, communal organization, parochial education, and, perhaps, also ties with a national ancestral country. Other elements, however—especially religious ones—are universal and equally relevant to all faiths because they are products, by the very definition of religion, of a divine or spiritual belief that is intended to respond to issues relating to the origin of human life and solutions to existential dilemmas (Robertson 1970).

Still, religious identity is multifaceted (Edgell 2012; Rebhun 2011). A major facet is the type of identity. Religious identity is composed of cognitive patterns (beliefs/attitudes) and instrumental behaviors (concrete acts; Christiano et al. 2008; James 1890; Buss and Finn 1987). Notably, according to the attitude-behavior theory (Fishbein and Ajzen 1975), these two types of identity are strongly related. Another facet of group identification is the venue, or environment, in which the individual demonstrates her or his identity: personal (private), interpersonal (public), or impersonal (transcendental). Personal identification reflects inner feelings or behaviors that an individual entertains at home or in a small family setting; the interpersonal stresses the collective manifestations of a religious identity; whereas the impersonal relates to attitudes or beliefs that focus on the cosmos. The distinction between these spheres, and especially between the personal and the interpersonal, becomes increasingly important over time as religion undergoes general privatization. Indeed, it is central to the controversy on the place of religion in present-day society (Casanova 1992; Gans 1994; Hartman and Hartman 2009; McGuire 2001). In each of the six combinations of categories of type of identification (cognitive, instrumental) and categories of the environment of identification (personal, interpersonal, impersonal), specific strategies of religious identification are invoked, such as rituals, community involvement, and values, to name only a few. Given the broad array of components of religious identification and their strong internal connections, the importance, or weight, of each component for assessing the overall strength of group identification may be different. In particular, instrumental behaviors are often more indicative of a group commitment than beliefs are. Behaviors require an investment of time, money, and involvement in institutions and interpersonal actions, whereas belief is a mere matter of one's feeling or outlook. This perception is supported by the empirical scalability of such fields as intergroup behavior and political involvement, which find beliefs to be at the lower end of the scale and overt actions at the top (Guttman 1959b; Levy 1985). Likewise, many empirical studies lead to the conclusion, albeit not a decisive one, that patterns of identification in the public sphere hold greater weight than those in the private sphere when it comes to assessing the overall group identification (DellaPergola 2001).

The discussion that follows assesses religious identification in the United States. Eighteen indicators are chosen (see appendix

A1) that reflect the various religious dimensions proposed. Each indicator relates to a single item in the Pew survey questionnaire. The responses are arranged to reflect religious commitment, from weak to strong. Attention is called first to the structure of religious identification, i.e., relations among the various indicators of religious identification, and further to the position of each religious group in this contextual array. Thereafter the religious groups are compared in relation to the intensity of identification along each of the religious indicators under examination; this should yield an assessment of Jewish identification vis-à-vis American religiosity in general and that of specific religious groups, both large and small, in particular. To complement the understanding of religious identification, a multivariate analysis is applied to deliver insights about the way socioeconomic attainment and family status—particularly intra- or intergroup marriages—weaken or strengthen religious identification, whether these factors operate similarly or differently on Jews and non-Jews, and how, after adjusting for individual sociodemographic characteristics, belonging to a given religious group influences its members' level of religious identification.

STRUCTURE OF RELIGIOUS IDENTIFICATION

A necessary first step in behavioral research, such as the study of religious identification, is the conceptualization and definition in substantive terms of the structure of the targeted population. This is done here through the application of an intrinsic (nonmetric) technique of facet theory (Guttman 1959a, 1968) that portrays coherent areas and boundaries of the relevant contents of religious identification. Religious identification is analyzed by mapping several clusters of engagement that the respondents expressed. The analysis also explores the proximity of each category of membership, namely group belonging, to the various identificational components.

Religious identification is defined by three facets (a facet being a set used for the classification of research issues; Levy 1985; Shye 1978). A suitable framework for defining the research variables, which simultaneously considers the classification of religious identity and its practical manifestations, is shown in the mapping sentence (figure 4.1). Facet A distinguishes between two modes of identification: cognitive (attitudes) and instrumental (behaviors). These modes are concerned with three domains (facet B), each reflecting a different orientation of religious identification among the American population: personal (primary internal), interpersonal (primary social), and impersonal (transcendental). These domains relate to contents of religion or ethnicity (facet C). Table 4.1 shows the name of each indicator (in alphabetic order) and how it relates to the mapping sentence. The table uses codes for the various facets; for example, $a_1b_2c_1$ indicates a cognitive behavior (attitude) oriented to interpersonal (primary social) relations of religious content. The response categories for each variable are worded in the sense of the specific attitude or behavior. Nevertheless, they should be interpreted in each case as ranging from low to high on a common concept of identification. This is specified in range facet R after the arrow in the mapping sentence.

To gain insights on the structure of the religious identification framework and the relationships between its components, the data are processed through a Smallest Space Analysis (SSA), which assesses the empirical correlational structure of variables

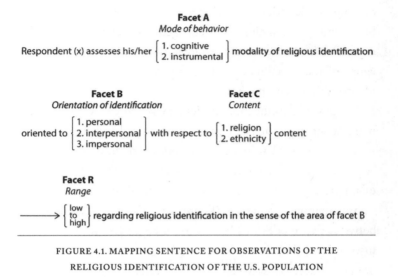

and produces a graphic translation of the matrix of correlation of all variables examined (Borg and Lingoes 1987; Guttman 1968). Each variable is represented as a point in a Euclidean space. The distance between a pair of points reflects the statistical similarity/ dissimilarity of the points: the stronger the correlation between two variables is—relative to the size of the correlation of either variable with other variables—the closer they are in the space. The points are distributed across the space of the smallest dimensionality that allows an inverse relation to exist between the observed correlations and the geometric distances, i.e., the order of the relations. Only the relative size of the correlations and distances are of interest.

When the relative sizes of the correlation coefficients are employed, SSA explores a representation that corresponds to a circular structure (figure 4.2). The circular space is partitioned

TABLE 4.1   INDICATORS OF RELIGIOUS IDENTIFICATION AND ASSOCIATED FACETS

Indicator	Code
Religion and politics (RELPOL)	cognitive, impersonal, community (a1b3 c2)
Origin of human life (EVOLHUM)	cognitive, impersonal, religion (a1b3c1)
Guidance on issues of right and wrong (RIGWRN)	cognitive, impersonal, community (a1b3c2)
Religious services (RELSERV)	instrumental, interpersonal, religion (a2b2c1)
Importance of religion (IMPREL)	cognitive, personal, religion (a1b1c1)
Participation in a choir (CHOIR)	instrumental, interpersonal, community (a2b2c2)
Community volunteer work (COMVOL)	instrumental, interpersonal, community (a2b2c2)
Work with children (CHILD)	cognitive, interpersonal, community (a1b2c2)
Participation in social activities (SOCACT)	cognitive, interpersonal, community (a1b2c2)
Membership in house of worship (MEMBER)	cognitive, interpersonal, community (a1b2c2)
Believe in God (BELV)	cognitive, personal, religion (a1b1c1)
View of God (VIEWGOD)	cognitive, personal, religion (a1b1c1)
Believe in life after death (LIFDET)	cognitive, personal, religion (a1b1c1)
Believe in heaven (HEAV)	cognitive, personal, religion (a1b1c1)
View of Bible/Holy Scripture (HOLYBK)	cognitive, personal, religion (a1b1c1)
Private prayer (PRAY)	instrumental, personal, religion (a2b1c1)
Participation in prayer group (PRAYGRP)	instrumental, interpersonal, religion (a2b2c1)
Read scripture (READSCRPT)	instrumental, interpersonal, religion (a2b2c1)

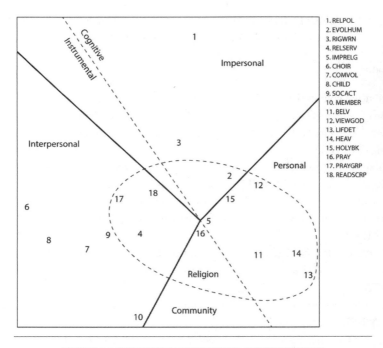

FIGURE 4.2. STRUCTURE OF RELIGIOUS IDENTIFICATION
IN THE UNITED STATES, 2007

into wedgelike regions that stem from a common origin, each corresponding to one of the environments introduced in facet B. A clear distinction exists between cognitive identification (attitudes) and instrumental identification (behaviors), each being in a delineating region in the right and left parts of the figure, respectively, marked by a broken line. Further, the facet of content of identification modulates between the religion and community, modulating the relative distance from the origin.

The orientation of identification facet divides the space into three regions emanating from an origin, each region turning in a different direction. Each region includes elements that coincide with the orientation of identification defined in facet B. Beginning in the upper part of the circle and proceeding clockwise, the regions are ordered as follows: impersonal, personal, and interpersonal. The circular order suggests that two points in the two-dimensional space that are equidistant from the origin but belong to different regions have a high correlation coefficient because the regions are statistically close to each other but may differ in content.

The mode of the content facet plays a modulating role. The distinction between religion and community partitions figure 4.2 into two major rings around the origin. Religious identificational variables are found in the inner circle; communal identificational variables are located in the outer ring. The shape of the inner region is an ellipse stretched between the two ends of the configuration, suggesting that different regions contain items that reflect behaviors and attitudes regarding the self. The item relating to the importance of religion in one's life appears in the center of the space; therefore, this variable may be interpreted as the most widely shared or "main" denominator of religious identification among different religious subpopulations in the United States.

Smallest Space Analysis allows external variables of attributes of the population, such as religious affiliation, to be integrated into the internal structure analysis—namely, the structure of the content—without affecting the internal structure (Cohen and Amar 2002). The SSA diagram maps the optimal location of each external variable by superimposing it on the structure of the examined topic of the total population. The external variables appear as dummy variables. Two groups, evangelical Protestants and Muslims, are the most closely associated with different paradigms of religious identification (figure 4.3). Both are located on the edge between the cognitive part of the configuration and the instrumental part. They are strongly oriented toward the impersonal. Other religious groups that claim a rather central location in the configuration are black Protestants, other Christians, other faiths, and Mormons. These groups, however, are located deep in the instrumental part, the one that is strongly associated with interpersonal relations. Jews are also found in that area, but somewhat on the fringe. Mainline Protestants and the unaffiliated are positioned at the two extremes of the configuration, meaning that they conceptualize the various patterns of religious identification in very different ways. In contrast, the proximity of Catholics and mainline Protestants indicates that they share a common orientation of personal religious activities. Still, Catholics are more closely associated with religious contents of identification, while mainline Protestants are located in the outer ring identified with communal contents of identification. These findings attest to the relevance, depth, and resilience of identification among different groups in the American population and illustrate how the entire identificational configuration is reconstituted through the combined performance of the ten theologically different religious groups.

The goodness of fit between observed coefficients and geometric distances is measured by the coefficient of alienation (Amar and Toledano 2001). This coefficient varies from 0 to 1, with 0 denoting a perfect fit (Borg and Lingoes 1987). The coefficient of alienation obtained for the configuration of religious identification is satisfactory at .13.

RHYTHM OF RELIGIOUS IDENTIFICATION

The level of religious identification is assessed in terms of the percent of members of each group who practice religious behaviors

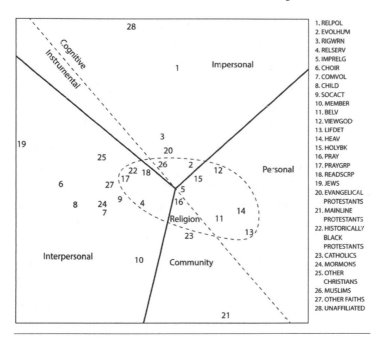

FIGURE 4.3. STRUCTURE OF RELIGIOUS IDENTIFICATION IN THE UNITED
STATES WITH RELIGIOUS GROUPS AS EXTERNAL VARIABLES, 2007

intensively or hold strong religious attitudes and beliefs. (The
definitions of "intensive" or "strong" are explained in the note to
table 4.2.) The data in the table show that the highest level of
religious identification that Jews attain (among all kinds of identification) is achieved by less than half of the population at large.
This proportion is attained for two behaviors: one in the public sphere, synagogue membership, and the other in the private
sphere, praying at least several times per month irrespective of the
performance of religious rituals.

Next in intensity are the various patterns of religious belief—
especially belief in God, the afterlife, and the existence of heaven.
For these, slightly more than four Jewish respondents in ten

responded in the affirmative. However, the views regarding God and the origin of the Bible are slightly weaker than those of religious belief. Internal variation was found among the religious pattern behaviors. While this variation may partly reflect differences in the importance of religious patterns for Judaism (a choir, for example, is not part of Jewish religious rituals), in others it attests to religious priorities among the many ways that individuals may choose to express their group identity. Still, the levels of religious behavior may be associated with sociodemographic characteristics such as age, marital status, and social and economic stratification; these are evaluated in the next section. As stated, the most common behaviors—those that characterize one of every two Jews—are synagogue membership and private prayer. The behavior that follows is participation in religious services, which typifies a little more than one-fourth of Jews. Roughly 15 percent of Jews take part in community social activities, participate in prayer groups, and read religious texts. Only one Jew in ten is involved in some form of voluntary community activity or, specifically, working with children.

Interestingly, only one-fourth of the Jews indicated that religion is something very important in their lives. This is half the rate of those who pray privately at least several times a month. Since an additional one-third of Jews indicated that religion is somewhat important to them, many of the latter also appear to engage frequently in private prayer. Another indicator of values, looking to religion for guidance on issues of right and wrong, characterizes only about 10 percent of Jews. This rate largely overlaps with the proportion who defined themselves as Orthodox, the religious hard core of the Jewish collective. It is more difficult to draw conclusions about the extent of religiosity from attitudes toward the origin of human life, even though those who disagree with evolution as the origin (16.8 percent) probably tend to have strong religious faith. About one-third of Jews believe that a house of worship should express views on current social and political issues. Insofar as such involvement is interpreted as a way of strengthening the role of religion in society, this rate is quite similar to the share of Jews who declared religion very important to them.[2]

Consistently across all indicators of Jewish identification, Jews by religion exhibit a stronger religious connection than ethnic Jews. The differences between these subpopulations are particularly evident in the importance of religion in the individual's life and in public community and religious activities. At the private level of religious behavior, namely prayer and religious beliefs, the distance between the two subpopulations is smaller. It bears emphasis that ethnic Jews are not necessarily estranged from Jewish religion and community; about one-fourth of them are fully confident that God exists, one-third believe in the afterlife, and slightly over one-fourth engage regularly in private prayer. Although people who adhere to these religious patterns may interpret them in ways that do not necessarily correspond to the Jewish religion, an important public manifestation of religious belonging—synagogue membership—characterizes almost two of ten ethnic Jews.

Religious identification is weaker among Jews than among non-Jews. The differences are especially large in attitudes on religious matters; in most of these patterns the level among Jews is one-third to one-half lower than that among non-Jews. The smallest difference between the populations, i.e., the strongest resemblance, is in membership in a house of worship: half the Jews and 62 percent of non-Jews are members. Still, across the range of indicators with few exceptions, Jews display the lowest level of religiosity among the religious groups (apart from the unaffiliated).

For each of the eighteen indicators of religious identification, the ten groups are ranked from 1 for the group that attained the highest percent to 10 for the group that earned the lowest. Thus, each group's total score may range from 18 (the strongest religiosity) to 180 (the weakest). On this scale, Mormons have the strongest religious identification. In thirteen of the eighteen indicators they ranked first. They are followed by black Protestants and then by evangelical Protestants. Each of these three groups scored less than 50. In the middle range are other Christians, Muslims, mainline Protestants, and Catholics, with average scores of 79–113. At the bottom of the scale are affiliates of other faiths, Jews, and the unaffiliated, with average scores of 147–168.

The scores yielded by the relative ranking of the groups may reflect large or small differences in religious identification. A detailed look at the percentages shows that the differences among the groups are large. In most indicators, the group that exhibits the strongest religiosity has at least twice as many members, proportionately speaking, who hold strong religious attitudes or practices than the least religious group. Small differences are found in three indicators: belief in God, belief in the afterlife, and frequent private worship. Overall, the findings reveal considerable disparity between the religious groups in levels of religiosity and show that Jews and the American Protestant and Catholic religious mainstreams are quite far apart in their religious faith and commitment.

THE SHAPING OF RELIGIOSITY

After examining the structure of religious identity and the levels of religious patterns, attention turns to the role of personal characteristics and group belonging in the shaping of religiosity. To

TABLE 4.2 LEVELS OF RELIGIOUS IDENTIFICATION AMONG JEWS AND OTHER RELIGIOUS GROUPS IN THE UNITED STATES, 2007 (PERCENTAGES AND SCORES)

	RELOPOL	EVOLHUM	RIGWRN	RELSERV	IMPREL
Total Jews	32.7 (9)	16.8 (10)	9.5 (8)	28.5 (9)	26.6 (9)
Jews by religion	34.6	18.4	10.3	32.1	30.7
Ethnic Jews	21.1	6.8	5.2	8.1	2.4
Total other religions	52.7	49.0	31.1	55.7	57.6
Evangelical Protestants	66.6 (2)	74.8 (2)	53.7 (2)	73.2 (3)	79.1 (3)
Mainline Protestants	48.0 (6)	49.3 (6)	24.5 (6)	54.2 (7)	52.0 (7)
Black Protestants	72.0 (1)	56.9 (4)	44.3 (4)	75.5 (2)	85.2 (1)
Catholics	50.0 (4)	37.7 (7)	23.2 (7)	61.0 (6)	56.4 (6)
Mormons	49.5 (5)	77.5 (1)	59.7 (1)	85.2 (1)	83.0 (2)
Other Christians	30.2 (10)	62.4 (3)	47.3 (3)	67.4 (4)	70.8 (4)
Muslims	54.8 (3)	53.3 (5)	33.5 (5)	61.3 (5)	67.4 (5)
Other faiths	33.1 (8)	18.3 (9)	5.8 (10)	32.6 (8)	40.1 (8)
Unaffiliated	36.3 (7)	24.0 (8)	5.9 (9)	10.3 (10)	16.2 (10)

	CHOIR	COMVOL	CHILD	SOCACT	MEMBER
Total Jews	2.6 (9)	10.6 (9)	8.3 (9)	16.1 (9)	50.1 (7)
Jews by religion	3.0	11.9	9.4	18.9	56.0
Ethnic Jews	0	2.7	1.5	0.8	16.1
Total other religions	11.8	19.2	18.8	28.9	62.0
Evangelical Protestants	18.1 (4)	26.7 (4)	27.5 (4)	43.8 (3)	74.3 (3)
Mainline Protestants	9.4 (5)	17.2 (6)	15.1 (6)	28.6 (6)	64.9 (6)

(*continued*)

	CHOIR	COMVOL	CHILD	SOCACT	MEMBER
Black Protestants	28.4 (1)	32.8 (3)	34.6 (2)	48.3 (2)	83.3 (2)
Catholics	7.2 (8)	15.8 (7)	14.1 (7)	20.2 (8)	67.5 (5)
Mormons	23.5 (3)	54.2 (1)	54.1 (1)	63.0 (1)	92.4 (1)
Other Christians	24.0 (2)	36.1 (2)	30.6 (3)	39.2 (4)	69.4 (4)
Muslims	7.3 (6.5)	23.7 (5)	24.2 (5)	34.3 (5)	41.9 (8)
Other faiths	7.3 (6.5)	14.4 (8)	12.9 (8)	20.8 (7)	31.1 (9)
Unaffiliated	2.0 (10)	3.7 (10)	4.6 (10)	5.6 (10)	22.0 (10)

	BELV	VIEWGOD	LIFDET	HEAV	HOLYBK
Total Jews	42.3 (9)	25.4 (10)	44.5 (10)	41.5 (10)	36.1 (8)
Jews by religion	44.8	27.4	46.1	44.3	41.7
Ethnic Jews	26.1	13.9	34.0	25.9	5.6
Total other religions	74.8	65.7	81.2	82.4	70.6
Evangelical Protestants	90.8 (2)	84.3 (2)	89.7 (2)	93.3 (3)	93.1 (2)
Mainline Protestant	74.6 (6)	67.9 (5)	84.8 (4)	86.6 (6)	68.7 (7)
Black Protestants	91.9 (1)	77.3 (3)	85.1 (3)	96.8 (2)	90.7 (3)
Catholics	73.6 (7)	65.1 (6)	83.7 (5)	89.0 (4)	69.7 (6)
Mormons	90.4 (3)	93.1 (1)	98.5 (1)	97.4 (1)	95.7 (1)
Other Christians	85.0 (4)	70.2 (4)	68.4 (8)	63.8 (7)	77.8 (5)
Muslims	84.8 (5)	45.0 (7)	81.3 (6)	88.6 (5)	88.8 (4)
Other faiths	54.2 (8)	30.1 (9)	75.9 (7)	42.1 (9)	22.3 (10)
Unaffiliated	39.9 (10)	30.8 (8)	55.6 (9)	47.5 (8)	28.7 (9)

	PRAY	PRAYGRP	READSCRPT	Sum of scores
Total Jews	50.7 (9)	16.5 (9)	17.4 (9)	162 (9)
Jews by religion	54.4	18.7	19.7	
Ethnic Jews	29.6	4.2	4.6	
Total other religions	82.2	32.5	46.1	
Evangelicals Protestant	95.4 (2)	53.5 (3)	71.5 (3)	49 (3)
Mainline Protestant	85.3 (6)	25.6 (6)	40.1 (6)	107 (6)
Black Protestants	95.9 (1)	57.7 (2)	74.3 (2)	39 (2)
Catholics	86.8 (5)	20.3 (8)	32.4 (7)	113 (7)
Mormons	95.2 (3)	73.8 (1)	83.0 (1)	29 (1)
Other Christians	91.2 (4)	50.4 (4)	61.1 (4)	79 (4)
Muslims	83.9 (7)	40.3 (5)	56.4 (5)	96.5 (5)
Other faiths	70.7 (8)	20.8 (7)	31.3 (8)	147.5 (8)
Unaffiliated	43.3 (10)	8.3 (10)	15.6 (10)	168 (10)

The levels of religious identification reflect the following responses: for RELPOL—should express views; for EVOLHUM—mostly/completely disagree; for RIGWRN—religious teaching and beliefs; for RELSERV—once or twice a month/once a week/more than once a week; for IMPREL—very important; for CHOIR—once or twice a month/at least once a week; for COMVOL—once or twice a month/at least once a week; for CHILD—once or twice a month/at least once a week; for SOCACT—once or twice a month/at least once a week; for MEMBER—yes; for BELV—absolutely certain; for VIEWGOD—God is a person; for LIFDET—yes; for HEAV—yes; for HOLYBK—word of God; for PRAY—a few times a month/once a week/a few times a week/once a day/several times a day; for PRAYGRP—once or twice a month/at least once a week; for READSCRPT—once or twice a month/at least once a week.

that end, the eighteen original variables are used to create a small number of measures of religious identification (by means of factor analysis). The first factor, "interpersonal instrumental," expresses activities and includes the following variables: social involvement, volunteer work, working with children, attendance at religious services, participation in prayer groups, participation in a choir, reading of Scripture, and membership in a house of worship. The second factor, "personal cognitive," reflects beliefs and attitudes: belief in heaven, God, the afterlife, importance of religion, private praying, view of God, and perception of Scripture. The third factor, "impersonal cognitive," includes the variables of religion as a source of guidance on issues of right and wrong, explaining the origin of human life, and involvement of house of worship in politics. Each of these variables represents a rather different aspect of religiosity and, accordingly, has a relatively low level of reliability.[3] By and large, the relations among the constituent variables of each factor correspond to the structure of religious identification as obtained in the facet analysis.

In accordance with the index nature of the measures of religious identification, the data were analyzed by means of ordinary least squares regression. The results indicate the direction (positive/negative) and the intensity of relations between an individual independent variable and the identification measure,[4] all other independent variables held constant. Here, as in previous chapters, separate models are presented for Jews, non-Jews, and integrated models for the American population at large that include group belonging as an independent variable.

Religious Activities: The Interpersonal Instrumental Perspective

Among Jews, very young age correlates positively with religious activity (table 4.3). It stands to reason that this is associated with a disproportional concentration of the Orthodox in this age bracket. The two intermediate age groups are not significantly different in the intensity of their religious activity relative to their elder peers.

Similarly, no differences in religious activity are found by gender as well as among the four main geographic regions. Living in suburban neighborhoods far from city centers deters religious activities. No significant relation is found between rural localities far from urban centers and less religiosity; this may reflect the intensive community nature and social cohesion that typify this form of residency, which also permeates the religious domain. Immigrants are less inclined than native-born to be religiously active. This finding is reinforced by the major origin of recent Jewish migration to the United States, the former Soviet Union. In the USSR, religion was prohibited and the authorities oppressed any expression of religious belief or practice. A much smaller proportion of immigrants arrived from Israel; they exhibit stronger religious and ethnic identification than native-born American Jews (Rebhun and Lev Ari 2010). While the Israeli immigrants may compensate for some of the FSU counterparts' negative effect on Jewish identification, they do not offset it totally. Indeed, religious and communal participation may provide recent immigrants with devotional guidance and protection for their spatial journey (Hagan and Ebaugh 2003); it may also replace the extended family as a source of social comfort and support (Cadge and Ecklund 2007). However, immigration may also entail social and economic adjustments that involve time and effort. These, together with social and cultural pressure from an unfamiliar environment, inhibit religious participation (Killian 2001), as appears to be the case with immigrant Jews in the United States.

Being unmarried—mainly single but also divorced or separated—is negatively associated with religious activity. The same is true for having a non-Jewish spouse as compared to religious endogamy. High social stratification acts in opposing directions: higher education enhances religious activity while high income deters it. Higher education equips one with civil qualifications that are needed for many kinds of organized participation; this, in turn, makes participation in religious organizations more likely (Schwadel 2011). Likewise, advanced schooling broadens intellectual horizons (Lehrer 1998) and, perhaps, strengthens individuals' awareness of and interest in group origins, hence religious activity. Furthermore, for well-educated people, religious activity—especially in the public domain—enhances social status and social capital (McFarland, Wright, and Weakliem 2011). Although high income eases organizational memberships and belonging, which often involve payment, it seems to have a stronger effect on channeling the individual's interests in the direction of economic and material affairs at the expense of group behaviors. Overall, sociodemographic characteristics explain nearly 12 percent of the variation in religious activity among Jews.

Among non-Jews, in contrast, young age mitigates religious activity; this is evident in all age cohorts relative to the sixty-five-plus group. Being female, living outside the Northeast, and living in rural localities—factors that did not play an important role among Jews—significantly strengthen religious activity among non-Jews. The other characteristics of foreign-born nativity status, marital status other than endogamy, and high socioeconomic stratification are associated with religious activity in a similar way among non-Jews and Jews. Notably, even though intermarriage has a negative effect on religious activities, the effect is slightly more moderate among non-Jews than among Jews. It is possible that many mixed marriages among non-Jews take place between members of different Christian denominations; accordingly, they exhibit a greater degree of religious compatibility (Lehrer 1998) than Jews do when they marry Christians. Along paths of dissimilarity between Jews and non-Jews in some of the relations and of similarity between them in others, the model was much less efficient in explaining the variance in non-Jews' religious activity—5.5 percent, only about half the explanatory power the same model found for Jews.

When Jews and non-Jews are pooled and religious belonging is presented as an independent variable, it is revealed that Jews are more predisposed to religious activity than non-Jews. The coefficient of this relation of .052 is statistically significant at p < .001. A detailed comparison by specific religious groups shows that Jews are less religiously involved than the reference group (mainline Protestants). Three other groups that are negatively associated with religious activity are, somewhat surprisingly, Catholics, followed by people of other faiths, and the unaffiliated; the latter have an especially strong negative correlation. The remaining religious groups exhibit stronger religious involvement than the reference group. The group that displays the strongest religiosity is the evangelical Protestants; religiosity among black Protestants and Mormons is also quite strong. Accordingly, from the standpoint of religious activity, and after adjusting for individual sociodemographic characteristics, Jews rank at the very bottom among America's main religious groups.

The breakdown by religious groups contributed meaningfully in explaining variance in religious activity. The explanatory power of model 4 is 30.3 percent, roughly six times greater than that of model 3, which draws a dichotomous distinction between Jews and non-Jews. The conclusion is that specific characteristics anchored in each religion, rather than a rough belonging to a category that aggregates several religious groups, are key in understanding differences in religious activities. Furthermore, specific group belonging does more to explain levels of religious activity than personal sociodemographic characteristics do.

TABLE 4.3 DIRECTION (POSITIVE/NEGATIVE)
AND MAGNITUDE OF THE EFFECTS
OF SOCIODEMOGRAPHIC CHARACTERISTICS
AND GROUP BELONGING ON INSTRUMENTAL
INTERPERSONAL RELIGIOUS IDENTIFICATION,
UNITED STATES, 2007

	Jews	Non-Jews	Total with group belonging	Total with religious identity
Age 18–29	0.342***	-0.057***	-0.050***	0.003
Age 30–44	0.187	-0.070***	-0.064***	-0.036***
Age 45–64	0.135	-0.035***	-0.032***	-0.020***
Female	0.040	0.098***	0.097***	0.060***
Midwest	-0.011	0.062***	0.059***	0.031***
South	0.034	0.189***	0.185***	0.086***
West	-0.039	0.022***	0.020***	-0.007
Suburban	-0.097***	-0.001	-0.003	-0.007
Rural	-0.038	0.053***	0.052***	0.041***
Foreign-born	-0.058*	-0.010*	-0.011**	0.027***
Single	-0.281***	-0.046***	-0.049***	-0.042***
Divorced/ separated	-0.099***	-0.071***	-0.072***	-0.070***
Widowed	-0.043	-0.016***	-0.016***	-0.022***
Intermarried	-0.174***	-0.062***	-0.064***	-0.096***
High school graduate	0.329***	0.018**	0.019***	0.026***
Some college	0.288***	0.062***	0.062***	0.066***
College graduate	0.392***	0.063***	0.063***	0.098***
Medium income	-0.078*	0.001	0.000	0.009*
High income	-0.047	-0.018***	-0.019***	-0.004
Very high income	-0.114*	-0.040***	-0.040***	-0.011**
Jews	–	–	0.052***	-0.055***

(*continued*)

(*continued*)

	Jews	Non-Jews	Total with group belonging	Total with religious identity
Evangelical Protestants	–	–	–	0.228***
Black Protestants	–	–	–	0.175***
Catholics	–	–	–	-0.030***
Mormons	–	–	–	0.151***
Other Christians	–	–	–	0.066***
Muslims	–	–	–	0.007*
Other faiths	–	–	–	-0.047***
Unaffiliated				-0.327***
% variance explained (adjusted R^2)	11.7%	5.5%	5.8%	30.3%

Note: *$p < .05$; **$p < .01$; ***$p < .001$; the numbers are standardized coefficients (beta) from an OLS regression; the reference categories are as follows: age—65+; gender—male; region of residence—Northeast; community of residence—urban; nativity status—native-born; marital status—married within the faith; education—primary/high school incomplete; earnings—low income; group belonging—non-Jews; religious identity—mainline Protestants.

Religious Beliefs: The Personal Cognitive Perspective

By and large, religious beliefs and religious activities are determined by different sets of factors. The main determinants of Jews' religious beliefs are age, whereas young people have stronger religious beliefs than older people, and gender, which attests to stronger belief among women than among men (table 4.4). Conversely, living in the South and having higher wages are negatively associated with faith. Nativity status, marital status (including intermarriage), and educational attainment, which show a significant relation with religious activity, are unimportant in determining the intensity of religious beliefs. Although only half as many variables have statistically significant effects on religious beliefs as on religious activity, the power of the former in explaining variance is greater at a level of 17.8 percent.

Among non-Jews, the direction and significance of the determinants of religious activities and religious beliefs are highly consistent. The young have weaker religious beliefs than the elderly; women have stronger beliefs than men. Living in the Midwest and the South, as well as in suburban and rural localities, enhances religious beliefs. The foreign-born are characterized by weaker beliefs than their American-born peers. The unmarried (single/divorced), as compared to being married (but not the intermarried), and those who have high income correlate negatively with religious beliefs. In the latter variable, the negative effect rises in tandem with income. Education weakens religious beliefs, possibly because the scientific foundations of higher education clash with some religious doctrines and beliefs—although this may vary across the range of religious traditions (in our case, Jewish versus non-Jewish; Schwadel 2011). Accordingly, while higher schooling strengthens involvement in communal institutions, this involvement is not necessarily guided by religious faith. Rather, it may reflect a group consciousness and identification that are perceived in terms of ethnicity, culture, and, more generally, a desire for organizational belonging. As with Jews, among non-Jews as well, sociodemographic variables are roughly twice as powerful in explaining differences in religious beliefs as in explaining differences in religious activities.

Adjusting for differences in sociodemographic characteristics, it is found that being Jewish per se enhances religious beliefs as compared with non-Jews. Group belonging is more important for religious beliefs than for religious activities, as evidenced by the size of the effects of being Jewish versus non-Jewish in tables 4.3 and 4.4. Yet, as with religious activities, Jews do not have an advantage over all religious groups; their religious beliefs are stronger only relative to the unaffiliated and are weaker than those of mainline Protestants. Groups that have stronger religious beliefs than mainline Protestants are evangelical Protestants, black Protestants, Catholics, Mormons, and Muslims. Consistent with previous insights, non-Jews are an agglomerate of very different religious groups in which the unaffiliated have much weight because of both their size and their deviation. Any dichotomy analysis in the study of American Jews and non-Jews masks important internal variations and group uniqueness among the latter population, lending support to the development of research from the lump approach to the split approach of detailed religious affiliation as is applied here.

The sociodemographic and group belonging variables manage, together, to explain 43.4 percent of the variance in religious beliefs—a very satisfactory level of power for a model that aims to explain differences in individual behavior. As with religious activities, it is very helpful to decompose non-Jews into specific groups in order to understand differences in levels of religious faith.

Transcendence: The Impersonal Cognitive Perspective

As stated, the impersonal dimension of religiosity is composed of three variables that forfeit some of their reliability when merged into a single index. Nevertheless, this index yields several important complementary insights for the assessment of religious identification of Jews versus non-Jews. First, as with the two

TABLE 4.4 DIRECTION (POSITIVE/NEGATIVE)
AND MAGNITUDE OF THE EFFECTS OF
SOCIODEMOGRAPHIC CHARACTERISTICS AND
GROUP BELONGING ON PERSONAL COGNITIVE
RELIGIOUS IDENTIFICATION, UNITED STATES, 2007

	Jews	Non-Jews	Total with group belonging	Total with religious identity
Age 18–29	0.284***	-0.082***	-0.072***	0.008
Age 30–44	0.289***	-0.039***	-0.030***	0.016**
Age 45–64	0.238***	-0.010	-0.003	0.023***
Female	0.203***	0.167***	0.166***	0.117***
Midwest	-0.021	0.072***	0.069***	0.049***
South	0.069*	0.167***	0.162***	0.089***
West	-0.057	0.005	0.004	0.004
Suburban	-0.016	0.022***	0.021***	0.003
Rural	-0.024	0.045***	0.043***	0.026***
Foreign-born	0.003	-0.051***	-0.049***	-0.035***
Single	-0.047	-0.065***	-0.063***	-0.049***
Divorced/ separated	0.024	-0.040***	-0.038***	-0.034***
Widowed	-0.005	0.000	0.001	-0.005
Intermarried	-0.039	0.007	0.006	-0.041***
High school graduate	0.101	-0.016*	-0.014*	-0.009
Some college	-0.060	-0.017**	-0.017**	-0.019***
College graduate	-0.086	-0.100***	-0.100***	-0.065***
Medium income	0.008	-0.033***	-0.032***	-0.025***
High income	-0.030	-0.059***	-0.057***	-0.051***
Very high income	-0.230***	-0.089***	-0.092***	-0.071**
Jews	-	-	0.128***	-0.146***
Evangelical Protestants	-	-	-	0.154***

(continued)

(*continued*)

	Jews	Non-Jews	Total with group belonging	Total with religious identity
Black				
Protestants	–	–	–	0.084***
Catholics	–	–	–	0.017***
Mormons	–	–	–	0.087***
Other				
Christians	–	–	–	-0.005
Muslims	–	–	–	0.017***
Other faiths	–	–	–	-0.110***
Unaffiliated				-0.486***
% variance explained (adjusted R²)	17.8%	9.5%	11.7%	43.4%

* p < .05; ** p < .01; *** p < .001; the numbers are standardized coefficients (beta) from an OLS regression; the reference categories are as follows: age—65+; gender—male; region of residence—Northeast; community of residence—urban; nativity status—native-born; marital status—married within the faith; education—primary/high school incomplete; earnings—low income; group belonging—non-Jews; religious identity—mainline Protestants.

previous indexes, the sociodemographic variables explain a larger share of variance in Jews' impersonal religiosity than in that of non-Jews (table 4.5). Second, being Jewish is positively and significantly associated with the impersonal dimension of religiosity. Third, Jews are less inclined than members of the reference group (mainline Protestants) to display impersonal religiosity. According to the level of the correlations, Jews are near the bottom of the impersonal religiosity scale; only two groups, adherents of other faiths and the unaffiliated, have a stronger negative relation. As with the other indexes of Jewish identification, the differentiation

TABLE 4.5 DIRECTION (POSITIVE/NEGATIVE) AND MAGNITUDE OF THE EFFECTS OF SOCIODEMOGRAPHIC CHARACTERISTICS AND GROUP BELONGING ON COGNITIVE IMPERSONAL RELIGIOUS IDENTIFICATION, UNITED STATES, 2007

	Jews	Non-Jews	Total with group belonging	Total with religious identity
Age 18–29	0.231***	0.002	0.005	0.041***
Age 30–44	0.207***	0.023***	0.026***	0.042***
Age 45–64	0.038	0.024***	0.025***	0.029***
Female	0.128***	0.108***	0.107***	0.082***
Midwest	-0.102***	0.078***	0.073***	0.037***
South	0.068*	0.168***	0.161***	0.059***
West	-0.101***	0.041***	0.036***	0.011*
Suburban	-0.037	0.028***	0.026***	0.014***
Rural	0.038	0.065***	0.064***	0.040***
Foreign-born	-0.084**	-0.089***	-0.088***	-0.047***
Single	-0.225***	-0.069***	-0.071***	-0.050***
Divorced/ separated	-0.062*	-0.046***	-0.046***	-0.039***
Widowed	-0.062*	-0.014***	-0.015***	-0.018***
Intermarried	-0.121***	-0.049***	-0.050***	-0.058***
High school graduate	-0.002	0.025***	0.026***	0.035***
Some college	0.020	0.015*	0.015*	0.025***
College graduate	0.025	-0.055***	-0.054***	-0.010
Medium income	-0.067	-0.011*	-0.012*	-0.004
High income	-0.267***	-0.033***	-0.036***	-0.022***
Very high income	-0.416***	-0.071***	-0.075***	-0.047***
Jews	–	–	0.077***	-0.073***

(*continued*)

(*continued*)

	Jews	Non-Jews	Total with group belonging	Total with religious identity
Evangelical Protestants	-	-	-	0.305***
Black Protestants	-	-	-	0.115***
Catholics	-	-	-	-0.029***
Mormons	-	-	-	0.085***
Other Christians	-	-	-	0.022***
Muslims	-	-	-	0.016***
Other faiths	-	-	-	-0.097***
Unaffiliated				-0.207***
% variance explained (adjusted R²)	15.4%	6.6%	7.6%	26.1%

*p < .05; **p < .01; ***p < .001; the numbers are standardized coefficients (beta) from an OLS regression; the reference categories are as follows: age—65+; gender—male; region of residence—Northeast; community of residence—urban; nativity status—native-born; marital status—married within the faith; education—primary/high school incomplete; earnings—low income; group belonging—non-Jews; religious identity—mainline Protestants.

of non-Jews by specific group belonging increases the explanatory power of the model considerably.

Religious identification in the United States is coherently organized. Clear distinctions are made between cognitive and instrumental elements; among the personal, interpersonal, and impersonal dimensions; and by main areas of identification of state and society, cosmology, beliefs, activity, and values. Within this structure, the importance the individual attributes to religious faith is a significant point of departure for all other manifestations of religious identification. The various religious groups are scattered across different areas in the religious identification structure, with evangelical Protestants and Muslims occupying the part closest to the center, i.e., relatively close to the entire components of religious identification. Each given group may be proximate to another group or to several groups; in this respect, Catholics and mainline Protestants, on the one hand, and the unaffiliated, on the other, are at the extremes of the configuration, demonstrating the gulf that separates them in religious identification. Jews are the closest to black Protestants and other Christians. This position attests to the Jews' emphasis, stronger than that of other groups, on behaviors more than attitudes and on interpersonal behaviors over personal patterns.

Along the identification patterns, Jews by religion exhibit stronger religious commitment than ethnic Jews. In comparison with other American religious groups, Jews obtain lower scores that, by and large, rank them second from the bottom only to the unaffiliated. Especially large differences between Jews and non-Jews are found in cognitive patterns; the differences are smaller in instrumental behaviors. This is manifested, among other things, in synagogue membership and private prayer as the two most frequent identification patterns among Jews. Whereas Jews are positioned near the bottom in the strength of their religious identification, the top is occupied by Mormons, black Protestants, and evangelical Protestants. Insofar as it was possible to compare Jews in 2007 and in 2013 (with the help of the Pew survey of the American Jewish population from the latter year), they very likely continue to occupy a low rung on the American religious identificational ladder.

The Jews' low standing should be understood in the context of their sociodemographic profile. Specifically, the Jews' low marriage rate, preference of suburban lifestyle, and high economic stratification deter religious beliefs and practices. Were they more similar to their non-Jewish counterparts in these key social characteristics, their religious identification would probably be much stronger. The Jews' structural adjustment, which has evolved into social patterns somewhat unique compared to those of other Americans, has resulted in the weakening of religious commitment. Jews are likely to exhibit weaker identification than mainline Protestants as well as evangelical Protestants, black Protestants, Mormons, other Christians, and Muslims. They tend to identify more strongly only than the unaffiliated and, to some extent, as strongly as members of other faiths. Viewed across the entire religious spectrum, the findings demonstrate the importance of sociodemographic variables, religious group belonging in particular, for understanding differences in the rhythm of religious identity in the United States.[5]

5

POLITICAL ORIENTATION

RELIGION AND POLITICS

THE SPECTRUM of mainstream political, social, and economic worldviews and ideologies that contemporary America presents may be arranged on a continuum from liberalism to conservatism. Each outlook, liberal or conservative, has moderate, radical, and in-between variants that their adherents define as centrist or moderate. Either way, ideology as an attitudinal structure serves to interpret and construct political reality.

The most significant way people express their political and social outlook is through voting behavior. This, in turn, is guided by three main considerations. They are regarded as the sociological, psychological, and rational-choice perspectives (Antunes 2010; Arzheimer and Falter 2008; Bartels 2010; Knoke 1974; Van der Eijk and Franklin 2009). The sociological approach claims that people vote in accordance with their social class (Andersen and Heath 2000; Barnes and Kaase 1979; Brooks, Nieuwbeerta, and Manza 2006; Lazarsfeld, Berelson, and Gaudet 1944; Knutsen 2006). Voters consider the party, or candidate, that can most appropriately represent the interests involved in their group affiliation. Accordingly, group identities influence attitudes and interests, and these, in turn, determine how people vote. The psychological approach postulates that voters are expressive and not instrumental (Andersen and Heath 2000; Burden and Klofstad 2005; Greene 2004; Sanders 2003; Weisberg and Greene 2003). Individuals' political orientations are shaped in early stages of life and are influenced mainly by the family (Campbell and Kahn 1952; Converse 1964). Thus party loyalty is stable over time. This has been proven empirically, above all in countries that have a two-party political system such as the United States (Green and Palmquist 1990). The rational-choice approach, like the sociological one, is instrumental, but attributes importance to individual considerations (Edlin, Gelman, and Kaplan 2007). Drawing a parallel between political preferences and economic behavior, it argues that people vote in an attempt to maximize their personal social and economic gains (Downs 1957). Individuals carry out a profit-and-loss analysis not only of the parties' platforms but of how well they believe the parties are able to implement the individuals' favored policies (Olson 1965).

By and large, one may regard religious belonging as being anchored in the sociological approach. The nexus of religion and politics hinges on strong awareness among group members of their distinct identity relative to peers who belong to other religious denominations (Manza and Wright 2003; Wilcox, Jelen, and Leege 1993). Religious faith, as a construct of values and ethical codes, provides adherents with guidance of proper behavior within the secular domain, hence also political orientations (Wald 2003). Major public policy issues that mediate between religious faith and political patterns include education, gender equality, family values, abortion, social justice, and homosexuality, to name only a few. Thus an important distinction among religious affilia-tions is seen through the prism of families of denominations, e.g., Protestants, Catholics, Jews, and other main confessions.

Another important parsing that sheds light on political pref-erences is between those who consider religion important and those who do not (Kellstedt 1993). Strong religious commitment provides resources, namely, faith, institutions, and social networks, that stimulate political involvement and sharpen social attitudes (Wald 2003). People who have a religious worldview exhibit strong commitment and motivation; they believe that they are fulfilling a divine will. When their conviction is encouraged by a church, it will have a perceptible effect on individual political patterns. Among the various indicators of such a commitment, perhaps the most important one is participation in worship. This is because houses of worship, particularly in the United States, have a very powerful organizational structure of leadership, committees, and publications; as such, they can recruit members and use them very effectively to influence political affairs. Likewise, a house of wor-ship integrates believers into social networks that promote trust, cooperation, and exchange of information among individuals that facilitate involvement in public life, including political matters (Putnam 2000). Hence according to level of religiosity, but also depending on the frequency of interaction in social structures, religious groups may have different levels of political cohesion, ranging from overweighting on one side of the political spectrum to a relatively smooth distribution across liberal, moderate, and conservative sectors (Huckfeldt and Sprague 1995).

This chapter traces and seeks to understand the political lean-ings of American Jews. Its point of departure, as many studies have shown consistently, is that American Jews tilt toward liberalism. Accordingly, explanations for this political preference, anchored in specific group considerations, are provided first. Then Jews' voting patterns in the twentieth century and up to the 2012 elections are reviewed. To assess Jews' political tendencies, they are compared with those of Americans at large and with members of main religious groups through the medium of preference for Democratic or Republican candidates in the 2004 presidential contest. This discussion is accompanied by an analysis of the determinants of political voting, including demographic and socioeconomic indicators, ethnoreligious identification, and group belonging, hence shedding light on American Jews' considerations when casting their ballots in national political elections. Notably, even though the focus here is mainly on political voting (a behavior), political attitudes are targeted for attention as well. These two dimensions are strongly interrelated. Indeed, a preliminary examination found, as expected, that a large majority of Democratic voters define themselves as liberal, whereas those who cast ballots for Republican candidates define themselves in greater part as conservative.

AMERICAN JEWISH LIBERALISM

Traditionally, Jews have played an active if not prominent role in the leadership of American liberal and socialist movements and parties. A significant proportion of American Jews adhere to a political ideology that affirms liberalism or leans toward the socialist left. The deep roots of Jewish liberalism and its part in the Jewish self-definition spanned the entire twentieth century (Dollinger 2000; Forman 2001; Kammen 1986; Levy 1995). Notably, the social-democratic wing of the labor movement was once heavily backed by some urban Jewish sectors in the electorate (Howe 1976; Liebman 1979); more relevant among later generations is the left-leaning wing of the Democratic Party. Insights from the 2007 Pew Survey show that 42 percent of Jews described themselves as liberal or very liberal as against 21 percent of non-Jews; slightly less than one-fifth defined themselves as conservative/very conservative; and the remaining 39 percent professed moderate political views.

Although there is a broad consensus about the liberal profile of most American Jews, social scientists differ about how to interpret it (Feingold 2014). One theory explains it in terms of historical development, in that the contents of this ideology served the Jews well in the practical sense (Cohen 1958; Kaplan 2009; Walzer 1986). Ever since the French Revolution, Jews have found their allies in liberal circles, as they did in circles of the radical socialist left that developed from the late nineteenth century onward in both Europe and the United States. Given their diasporic experience as guests in host societies, Jews understood that they could best advance under liberal regimes that allow achievement to determine social and economic mobility and ban discrimination by law. Classical liberalism emphasizes the principle of individualism, which legitimizes the rights of minorities, including Jews, and encourages their full social integration. Given that liberalism also rests at the core of the American ethos, loyalty to its principles provides Jews with the means to prove their full identification with the United States.

A second theory sees the source of Jewish liberalism in religious values. Three basic principles connect the Jewish religion with the social agenda: study of canonical religious texts, which may help promote intellectualism and eventually may legitimize cultural relativism, universalism, and tolerance; charity as a Jewish imperative, which in modern times may entail support for the welfare state, minority rights, and progressive taxation; and a this-worldly theological emphasis, which fosters activism and the desire to shape and improve society (Fuchs 1956). More generally,

Jewish values and the religious characteristics of daily Jewish life are strong predictors of liberalism (Legge 1995).

The third explanation is sociological, and it suggests that the source of Jewish liberalism lies in the dissonance between the Jews' high socioeconomic attainments and their limited social acceptance ("status inconsistency"; Lenski 1961; Lipset 1960). This dissonance in status creates a feeling of marginality, which translates into support for liberal and even radical movements that challenge the social order and the cultural establishment oppressing them. Even though Jewish integration and acceptance in general society have been advancing steadily over time, the overwhelming majority of Jews perceive some extent of anti-Semitism in the country (Rebhun 2014) and under certain circumstances, such as the Pollard affair (Avineri 1987) or the more recent lifting of Iran sanctions (Kredo 2015), are afraid of being accused of dual loyalty.

According to the fourth theory of the Jews' political socialization, Jews view pro-liberalism as a historic lesson that they pass on from one generation to another. "We propose that the contemporary ideology of Jewish elites is a product of political socialization. Jewish liberalism is part of a family of liberalism that developed in response to European conditions. The tradition persists despite the changes that have taken place in American society in recent years" (Lerner, Nagai, and Rothman 1989:331). The transmission takes place through the primary agent of socialization, the institution of the family. And if the elites identify with a liberal outlook even though their socioeconomic status makes for interests that occasionally clash with it, all the more so for other social classes.

The fifth theory is sociocultural; it interprets liberalism as the reaction of Jews who want the option of education and modernity but reject its implications (Liebman 1973). The source of Jewish liberalism lies in the values of those Jews who, while alienated from the religious tradition, find themselves interacting with other Jews—an interaction that plays an important role in their liberalism. The Jewish commitment is not toward liberalism, which carries a message that is essentially one of internationalism, welfare society policies, and civil liberties, but toward enlightenment and the optimistic belief that human reason can create a good and progressive society that denies religion a role in decisions of state.

Yet another theory places Jews' political behavior within the frame of perceived Jewish political interests (Medding 1977). These include micropolitical interests, namely survival (in the case of American Jews, primarily the physical existence of the State of Israel), full participation in social life, religious freedom, patterns of particularistic group organization, and economic interests corresponding to the Jews' occupational structure, along with macropolitical interests, those relating to issues of legislation and organization of the social order in a way that will allow the micropolitical interests to be realized and sustained.

TRENDS IN JEWISH POLITICAL ORIENTATION AND VOTING PATTERNS

How does the liberal ideology of American Jewry find expression in political action and voting patterns in presidential elections? American Jews' political preferences in the twentieth century were fashioned largely by domestic political developments (Rosenberg and Howe 1976). Notably, Jews are a very politically aware group; their rate of participation in presidential elections (80 percent) is much higher than that of the general population (50 percent). Thus Jewish voters account for about 4 percent of the total electorate even though their proportion in the overall population is only about 2 percent (Fischer 1981). Moreover, the concentration of Jews in the six most populous states, those with the largest numbers of electoral votes (New York, California, New Jersey, Florida, Illinois, and Pennsylvania), amplifies the importance of the Jewish vote and turns the Jews into a sector to be courted by politicians. Jews amass economic power by contributing to political parties, and their focal positions in the shaping of public opinion—in teaching, written and electronic media, and the legal and political systems—strengthen their position as an influential political factor (Fischer 1981; Lefkowitz 1993).

The proportion of Jews who voted for the Democratic Party increased steadily after World War I and peaked in the 1930s and 1940s at 90 percent for Franklin Delano Roosevelt (Weisberg 2012). At that time the Democratic Party platform corresponded to Jewish interests in both foreign policy (involvement in World War II and, later, support for the establishment of Jewish statehood) and domestic policy (massive involvement in social and economic life and laying the foundations for the modern welfare state). A liberal-democratic coalition comprising various ethnic groups, including Jews, blacks, and Italians, developed around the common interest of protecting weaker members of society and helping marginal groups. During the early 1960s, cooperation and an alliance between Democratic Jews and blacks gathered strength in connection with the struggle for civil rights.

In all elections from 1932 on (with the exception of those in 1980, after President Jimmy Carter's term), 60–90 percent of American Jews voted for the Democratic candidate. In every election from 1924 on, Jews favored Democrats by about 20 percentage points more than the rest of the population did (Jewish Virtual Library, "Politics"; Lefkowitz 1993; Pew Research Center 2004). True, Jewish support for the Republican Party increased considerably in the 1972 elections, with 35 percent of Jews voting for Richard Nixon at the end of his first term as president, during which he demonstrated a sympathetic approach to Israel. Still, the Democratic candidate, George McGovern, received the majority of the Jewish vote.

Jewish support for the Democratic Party has been declining somewhat since the late 1960s. Several factors brought this about: 1. awareness among African Americans has grown, as has tension with whites in general, including Jews, over issues of quotas, affirmative action, and meritocracy (Lipset 1972; Rosenberg and Howe 1976); 2. the crisis in secular liberal thought after World War II and the turn toward extreme leftism, as opposed to traditional liberalism, were involved in the growth of the New Left. The American left as a whole was flooded by radical anti-establishmentarian elements and distanced itself from Jews to the point of hostility toward Jewish interests (including Israel after the Six-Day War, which was now perceived as an affluent state that obtained substantial economic and political resources from the United States and its Jews) and growing sympathy for the Arabs and Palestinians, now seen as weak, unfortunate, and underdeveloped (Lipset 1971); 3. the ascent of the New Right and the religious right, whose pro-Israel bias saw the state in religious terms as a bastion of opposition to the undemocratic Arab world alongside an alliance with the United States in its struggle against communism; 4. the breakdown of the liberal-Democratic coalition, dating back to Roosevelt and the New Deal, that had served as the basis for consensus and cooperation in the liberal camp around the cause of a socialist-oriented social policy (Kristol 1988); 5. a growing number of independent candidates, most of whom were breakaways from the Democratic Party (Schneider 1981); 6. the increasing reliance of Jewish liberal voters on Political

Action Committees (PACs) and other grassroots forms of political cal mobilization (Ginsberg 2001) rather than on Jewish Democratic members of Congress and Senate or state governors; and 7. the recent slow but steady growth of the Orthodox and ultra-Orthodox sector (Pew Research Center 2013; Rebhun 1993), which tends to vote conservative and may offset some of the more historically traditional Jewish sympathy for the Democrats.

Despite these tendencies, some of which were related to more transient developments in the overall social and economic configuration of the United States, a solid majority of American Jews remained in the Democratic camp. Other ethnic and age groups made much more vigorous moves toward the Republican Party. The fluctuations in the political support of American Jews were influenced by worries about support for Israel, racial politics, and the empowerment of religion in public life. The growth in Jewish support for the Republican Party that began in 1972 declined between 1980 and 2000. The 1996 and 2000 presidential elections gave evidence of the ongoing liberal tendency in that eight of every ten Jews cast their votes for the Democratic presidential candidate. The sense of relative security in American Jewish life did not weaken the perceived need to support universal interests of equality and social justice. Alternatively, one may argue that, despite their social integration, the Jews remain highly aware of belonging to a uniquely defined subgroup, perhaps involving some degree of uncertainty about "the security of their own achievements" as well as "skepticism regarding the Republican Party's willingness to accept as permanent the Civil Rights Revolution" (Kristol 1990:112). The 2004 elections revealed a slight change of direction in Jewish political preferences: 25 percent of Jewish voters cast their ballots for George W. Bush, up from 19 percent in 2000 (Pew Research Center 2004). The candidacy of an

African American man, Barack Obama, did not augur a possible change in Jewish political behavior: in 2008 the Republican candidate, John McCain, gained the support of 22 percent of American Jews, against 78 percent who voted for Obama (Weisberg 2012). Jewish support for the Republican candidate increased in the 2012 elections, as 30 percent of American Jews preferred Mitt Romney as against 69 percent who voted for the incumbent president, Obama (Pew Research Center 2012). Future presidential elections will show whether this was a passing phenomenon, reflecting support for Bush's antiterror policies and subsequent dissatisfaction with Obama's Middle East policy during the latter's first term, or a real shift in Jewish political behavior associated with structural changes—growing proportions of Orthodox and intermarried Jews along with changes in self-interest toward more materialistic economic and specific public policies (Windmueller 2003).

JEWS AND NON-JEWS IN THE 2004 PRESIDENTIAL ELECTIONS

The 2004 U.S. presidential elections were the last preceding the 2007 Pew survey. In those elections the Republican candidate and incumbent president, George W. Bush, ran against the Democratic rival, John Kerry. There were roughly ten additional candidates, each listed on the ballot in several states; the most prominent independent candidate was Ralph Nader. Only the candidates of the two major national parties, the Republican and Democratic, were registered in all fifty states and in Washington, DC.

In the 2004 elections, about two-thirds of the Jews voted for the Democratic candidate, Kerry; slightly more than one-fourth preferred Bush; and about 6 percent chose an independent candidate (figure 5.1). There were perceptible differences among the

Jews. Data not presented here show that more than twice as many Jews by religion voted for Bush as ethnic Jews—30 percent and 14 percent, respectively. Conversely, the rates of support for Kerry were 64 percent among Jews by religion and nearly 80 percent among ethnic Jews. (A similar proportion of members of both groups voted for other candidates.) By implication, a Jewish religious outlook is associated with political conservatism and a secular perspective connects with liberalism.

Jews and non-Jews have different political preferences. Among the latter, only 40 percent gave their votes to Kerry and more than half voted for Bush. Non-Jews are slightly more inclined than Jews to vote for a candidate who does not belong to one of the two major parties. Other religious groups that demonstrate a salient preference for Democrats are Muslims, adherents of other faiths,

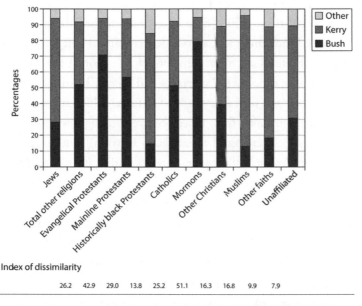

FIGURE 5.1. VOTING PATTERNS AMONG JEWS AND OTHER RELIGIOUS GROUPS IN THE 2004 U.S. PRESIDENTIAL ELECTIONS

and black Protestants: among all of them, an absolute majority (more than 50 percent) voted for Kerry. In fact, among the
ten religious groups, Jews are ranked fourth in the share of support for the Democratic candidate. At the other end of the scale,
Mormons, evangelical Protestants, and, to a somewhat smaller
but nevertheless salient extent, mainline Protestants and Catholics voted in greater part for George Bush. A large proportion of
black Protestants (16 percent) and one of every ten other Christians, adherents of other faiths, and unaffiliated persons voted for
an independent candidate. Thus people who have no affiliation
with a large religious faith or no religious belonging whatsoever
identify less with the mainstream political establishment.

The distribution of Jews' votes among Bush, Kerry, and the independent candidates most closely resembles the patterns of the religiously unaffiliated and adherents of other faiths. It is also rather
similar to those of black Protestants, Muslims, and other Christians. What these groups have in common is their distance from
the large Protestant and Catholic denominations and (in the case
of black Protestants) from the white racial majority. For some of
these groups, e.g., black Protestants and other Christians, average
social indicators (such as levels of educational achievement) appear
to differ significantly from those observed among Jews (as shown
in chapter 3). Therefore their similarity in voting patterns cannot
be attributed to structural characteristics; rather, it may stem from
minority status. This is not the case with regard to the disparity
between Jews and Muslims, whose differences in voting patterns
are very similar to the differences between them in educational
achievement (similar indexes of dissimilarity). Nevertheless, with
their high educational attainment, Jews tend more to vote Republican, whereas Muslims, who on average have lower levels of education, tilt toward Democrats. This may attest to the undermining of

Muslims' security, especially after the September 11 attacks and the sense that Democrats are more protective of and concerned about minorities. An analysis at the individual level may shed stronger light on the relations between structural characteristics (particularly education) as well as group belonging and political patterns.

SOCIODEMOGRAPHIC CHARACTERISTICS, RELIGIOUS IDENTIFICATION, AND VOTING PATTERNS

The clear preference of Jews for the Democratic Party, as reflected in the large proportion of votes for Kerry, is not indicative of all Jews equally. The distribution of Jews' votes between Kerry and Bush varied by sociodemographic characteristics and also by the intensity of their religioethnic identification. The differences among Jews by attribution to a specific category of a given variable may at times be small and at others quite large. Thus in several social or identificational categories most Jews (more than half) cast their ballots for the Republican candidate, Bush. Relations between individual characteristics and political preferences were also found among non-Jews.

Among Jews, those of middle age (thirty to forty-four) gave Kerry less electoral support than their younger and older peers did (table 5.1). Members of this age cohort are at a critical stage of their life cycle, a time of professional consolidation and family formation with all the needs that this brings in train, such as purchasing a house. It is possible that these personal challenges influence their socioeconomic worldview more strongly toward capitalism and favor the individual over the collective. Among non-Jews, in contrast, support for the Democratic candidate wanes in tandem with rising age. Accordingly, in the thirty to forty-four age cohort, the differences between Jews and non-Jews in the share of support for Kerry were less than 15 percent. The relation between age and political preferences among non-Jews is typical of most Christian religious groups (apart from evangelical Protestants and Mormons) and the unaffiliated, even if the decrease is sometimes disrupted by a momentary change in direction. There are no substantial gender differences in Jews' voting patterns. The same is true for non-Jews. Among both populations, women were slightly more in favor of Kerry than of Bush. This is reflected in all religious groups with the exception of other Christians. A higher voting rate for Kerry among women than among men stands out in particular among mainline Protestants, Muslims, and the religiously unaffiliated.

Jews at the two extremes of the American continent are quite different in their political preferences: those in the Northeast are less Democratic than those in the West. Among non-Jews, even though the differences are small, the relation is the opposite: more support for Kerry in the Northeast than in the West. The differences among non-Jews between Northeast and South are even greater, probably reflecting the large concentration of black Protestants in the latter region. Even among black Protestants, however, there are differences by region of residence: those in the Northeast are more Democratic than their peers in the West. Overall, Jews, Catholics, and Mormons share a positive relation between living in the West and strong support for the Democratic candidate, Kerry. A cluster of three other religious groups—other Christians, adherents of other faiths, and the unaffiliated—is particularly Democratic-oriented if its members live in the Northeast; evangelical Protestants, mainline Protestants, and black

Protestants have an especially strong preference for Kerry if they live in the Midwest; and, among Muslims, those in the South are exceptionally well disposed to Kerry. These observations attest to wide variations in the political orientations of religious groups in a given region of residence. Examination of a complementary geographic dimension, type of community, yields a different picture. Whereas suburban Jews exhibit a stronger Democratic affinity than their urban or rural peers, support for Kerry among non-Jews is strongest among urban dwellers. The latter pattern is true for all non-Jewish groups. (The high rate of support of Kerry among rural Muslims should be treated cautiously due to a very small sample size). Accordingly, the differences between urban Jews and urban non-Jews in political preferences are much smaller than those between Jews and non-Jews in suburban or rural areas.

Jewish immigrants to the United States lean toward political conservatism. Fewer than half of them voted for Kerry in the 2004 elections, possibly because many came from the former Soviet Union where they had spent decades living under rigid government control and supervision of all areas of personal life. Non-Jewish immigrants, in contrast, are more Democratic than their American-born peers. This pattern is typical of most religious groups, with one especially conspicuous outlier in black Protestants, whose pattern is reminiscent of that of the Jews.

Interestingly, intermarried Jews gave Kerry stronger support than Jews who married within the faith. More than adopting political patterns that typify non-Jewish Americans of the Republican persuasion, intermarriage alludes to an open and pluralistic worldview and, evidently, weaker religious self-identity, suggesting a better fit with a liberal social and political platform. This, however, may embody the effects of other factors associated with intermarriage such as young cohorts (which vote more Democratically) and regional distribution (with the intermarried tending to live outside metropolitan New York and, more generally, away from the Northeast and the Midwest). Similar relations between type of marriage (exogamy/endogamy) and political preferences were found among non-Jews in general and within most non-Jewish religious groups in particular. In this context, mainline Protestants demonstrated an opposite relation: endogamous members of this group were more Democratic than exogamous members were. The reason may be that mainline Protestants in mixed marriages are more likely than members of other religious groups in mixed marriages to have a Catholic spouse who tilts them toward a more religious and, accordingly, sociopolitically conservative, outlook. Almost without exception, singles are more likely than married people to vote for a Democratic presidential candidate.

Among Jews, educational attainment and political preference are strongly interrelated: the better schooled Jews were, the more they voted for Kerry. The differences between high-school dropouts and academic degree holders exceeded 30 percent. Among non-Jews the nexus of education and voting patterns is weak. Mainline Protestants and Catholics exhibit minor differences between the extremes of the educational ladder or fluctuations by levels of education. In contrast, black Protestants, adherents of other faiths, and the unaffiliated reveal patterns not far from those of the Jews. Among several other religious groups—especially evangelical Protestants, Mormons, and other Christians—the relations are the opposite, i.e., the better educated they are, the less they support Democrats. As for economic stratification, the relation with Jews' political voting is less consistent. Apparently, this may have to do with the somewhat arbitrary definition of the income categories. Still, when the two lowest-income groups are contrasted with the two highest-income groups, the latter prove to be less supportive of the Democratic Party. This connection is clearer and more consistent among non-Jews generally and among almost all non-Jewish religious groups separately.

Strong religious identification weakens support for the Democratic Party. This is reflected both in attitude (importance of religion) and in behavior (participation in religious services) and presents among Jews and non-Jews alike. Those who have the strongest religious identification gave Kerry about half the support that those with the weakest religious identification gave him. Among non-Jewish groups, the relation between religious identification and political voting is, by and large, more robust vis-à-vis the importance of religion than vis-à-vis the frequency of participation in religious services. For evangelical Protestants, mainline Protestants, and the unaffiliated, the relation between participation in religious services and voting behavior is also strong.

To sum up the similarities and dissimilarities between Jews and non-Jews, I indicated for members of each group the traits that are associated with the least voting for Kerry and those connected with the most (table 5.2). Five of ten traits act similarly among Jews and non-Jews in predicting weak support for Kerry: being male, living in a rural locality, religious endogamy, high level of religiosity (manifested in very high importance that the individual attributes to religion), and participation in religious services several times per week. Four traits shared by Jews and non-Jews correspond to strong support for Kerry: being female, having a college degree, and having very weak religious identification in both the importance of religion and the frequency of participation in religious services. Accordingly, gender and religious identification (both attitude and behavior) are factors that are most similarly associated with the voting patterns of Jews and non-Jews.

TABLE 5.1 VOTING PATTERNS (PERCENT VOTING FOR KERRY) BY MAJOR SOCIODEMOGRAPHIC CHARACTERISTICS AMONG JEWS AND OTHER RELIGIOUS GROUPS IN THE UNITED STATES, 2007

	Jews	Total other religions	Evangelical Protestants	Mainline Protestants	Black Protestants	Catholics	Mormons	Other Christians	Muslims	Other faiths	Unaffiliated
Age											
18–29	74.2	54.5	27.8	48.3	89.1	54.5	9.0	70.4	84.3	89.5	73.7
30–44	56.7	42.8	22.3	38.8	85.2	43.8	21.5	60.5	91.1	74.8	63.5
45–64	71.6	42.3	24.5	40.1	82.1	42.8	16.0	54.3	84.4	78.2	62.9
65+	77.0	38.5	25.9	35.3	72.4	42.7	15.9	44.2	60.0	79.1	61.6
Gender											
Male	68.5	40.9	24.2	35.3	81.4	41.1	14.0	57.3	80.0	78.6	60.0
Female	71.4	45.3	24.8	43.0	83.6	46.9	18.4	54.5	92.8	79.8	71.8

(continued)

	Jews	Total other religions	Evangelical Protestants	Mainline Protestants	Black Protestants	Catholics	Mormons	Other Christians	Muslims	Other faiths	Unaffiliated
Region of residence											
Northeast	64.4	48.0	26.6	40.7	83.3	44.8	32.1	65.9	90.9	87.7	71.0
Midwest	75.2	45.5	28.5	44.3	88.5	44.9	27.4	47.8	86.8	83.1	64.8
South	70.6	38.5	23.4	33.5	81.7	36.8	13.9	46.3	95.2	75.4	61.7
West	76.6	44.3	21.1	42.0	73.6	51.2	71.4	60.1	66.7	74.7	64.8
Community type											
Urban	66.3	53.7	32.0	44.5	85.2	50.5	26.4	59.0	91.7	81.1	74.0
Suburban	72.8	40.1	21.7	39.0	83.0	41.5	13.1	53.8	77.2	78.3	60.3
Rural	65.9	34.9	23.2	34.5	71.0	40.6	10.3	53.8	100.0	76.1	57.4
Nativity status											
Native-born	72.1	42.6	24.3	39.1	83.1	43.5	16.0	56.3	84.4	80.8	64.7

(continued)

(continued)

Foreign-born	47.1	55.4	33.6	53.1	67.6	52.6	29.0	51.9	87.3	70.8	71.9

Education

Primary/HS incomplete	41.9	45.1	29.8	40.6	77.0	52.3	31.6	59.4	100.0	67.6	58.4
HS graduate	58.8	40.0	26.1	35.6	82.3	41.9	16.9	60.4	100.0	69.1	55.4
Some college	68.8	41.3	24.0	35.4	83.8	42.9	15.4	58.2	82.5	72.8	63.2
College graduate	73.0	47.2	20.8	44.6	85.7	45.6	15.6	51.2	84.8	85.4	73.5

Income

Low	70.8	49.1	32.1	42.4	82.3	51.3	21.7	53.5	100.0	84.8	70.1
Medium	75.6	44.8	25.8	41.6	84.9	47.2	18.4	60.2	81.3	74.2	62.8
High	65.2	41.5	22.0	38.4	82.0	43.9	13.0	61.2	78.4	78.2	65.6
Very high	69.8	40.6	18.3	38.6	82.6	38.9	18.8	53.3	88.9	81.3	64.3

(continued)

(continued)

	Jews	Total other religions	Evangelical Protestants	Mainline Protestants	Black Protestants	Catholics	Mormons	Other Christians	Muslims	Other faiths	Unaffiliated
Income											
Low	70.8	49.1	32.1	42.4	82.3	51.3	21.7	53.5	100.0	84.8	70.1
Medium	75.6	44.8	25.8	41.6	84.9	47.2	18.4	60.2	81.3	74.2	62.8
High	65.2	41.5	22.0	38.4	82.0	43.9	13.0	61.2	78.4	78.2	65.6
Very high	69.8	40.6	18.3	38.6	82.6	38.9	18.8	53.3	88.9	81.3	64.3
Marital status											
Single	71.1	61.8	38.4	56.3	88.0	55.4	25.7	66.2	89.7	89.6	75.3
Divorced	80.0	47.8	30.5	40.7	77.4	52.2	18.8	64.2	52.2	79.9	61.7
Widowed	78.7	40.6	26.2	35.3	79.4	45.3	15.0	46.5	100.0	78.7	67.2
Inter-married	69.3	42.6	26.6	13.6	82.8	41.5	29.5	51.5	100.0	78.8	–
In-married	66.4	38.5	20.9	36.1	82.0	40.3	13.9	52.9	89.9	72.7	62.5

(continued)

Importance of religion

Not at all	87.4	68.5	39.2	51.0	100.0	53.7	12.5	94.1	80.0	87.4	71.4
Not too	80.5	58.7	40.9	44.7	80.5	59.5	40.9	72.7	100.0	82.5	65.7
Somewhat	70.2	48.1	37.9	43.3	85.1	46.9	40.8	55.8	80.0	78.8	60.2
Very	50.9	36.0	21.3	35.5	82.2	40.2	13.1	50.0	86.5	75.9	54.0

Attend religious services

Never	87.7	61.0	37.2	46.9	90.7	54.5	41.7	58.8	72.0	75.0	67.4
Seldom	55.7	55.7	35.4	43.4	87.7	55.4	34.5	74.6	100.0	81.8	66.2
Few times a year	67.3	47.1	36.0	39.7	90.3	46.1	16.1	58.3	80.0	76.1	62.3
1–2 a month	68.5	45.1	30.2	41.5	86.6	44.3	32.9	62.2	100.0	85.6	69.2
Once a week	50.6	35.8	21.5	35.9	84.2	40.4	14.5	37.8	76.9	84.3	47.9
More than once a week	35.8	29.1	16.7	33.5	74.8	34.3	12.3	53.2	100.0	72.3	30.8

TABLE 5.2 CHARACTERISTICS OF JEWS AND NON-JEWS WITH LOWEST AND HIGHEST VOTING FOR CANDIDATE KERRY IN THE 2004 PRESIDENTIAL ELECTIONS

	Lowest		Highest		
	Characteristics	Number of similar characteristics of Jews and non-Jews (out of 10)	Characteristics	Number of similar characteristics of Jews and non-Jews (out of 10)	
Jews	Age 30–44; male; residing in Northeast; in a rural locality; of foreign nativity; married within the faith; high school not completed; high income; stating religion is very important; and attending religious services more than once every week.		Age 65 and over; female; living in the West; in a suburban area; of American nativity; divorced (or separated); with an academic diploma; medium income; no importance at all of religion; and not attending religious services at all throughout the year.		

(continued)

(continued)

| Non-Jews | 5 | Age 65 and over; male; residing in the South; in a rural locality; of American nativity; married within the faith; graduated from high school; very high income; stating religion is very important; and attending religious services more than once a week. | 4 | Age 18–29; female; living in the Northeast; in an urban locality; of foreign nativity; being single; with academic diploma; low income; no importance at all of religion; and never attending religious services throughout the year. |

DETERMINANTS OF
VOTING BEHAVIOR

The differences in political preference according to social and identificational categories were not always consistent or meaningful. Likewise, it stands to reason that the relations between any given trait and voting entail other individual characteristics. To overcome these obstacles and provide a more refined insight into the relations between sociodemographic and religious identification characteristics and voting behavior, the data were analyzed through a multivariate approach (table 5.3).

Among Jews, being young, especially aged thirty to forty-four, inhibited voting for the Democratic presidential candidate. Living outside the Northeast correlated positively with Democratic voting. For example, those in the West were twice as likely to vote for Kerry as peers in the Northeast. Irrespective of region, living in a suburb increased the likelihood of support for Democrats relative to living in a city. All other things being equal, the foreign-born were significantly less Democratic, one-fourth as likely to vote for Kerry as the American-born. Neither marital status nor income is a significant determinant of Jews' political behavior. Education, however, was found to have an especially strong effect: persons with several years of college were three times as likely to vote for Kerry, and degree holders seven times as likely, as high school dropouts (the reference group). With the sociodemographic variables held constant, it was found that stronger religious identification deters voting for a Democratic presidential candidate. Although only a few variables showed a statistically significant relation, they managed to explain a high 29 percent of the variation among the Jews in support of Kerry as against support of Bush in the 2004 presidential elections.

To a large extent, the traits that link Jews with voting for the Democratic candidate have the opposite effect on non-Jews, i.e., prompt them to vote for the Republican candidate. The most conspicuous traits of this kind are young age and American nativity, which corresponded to voting for Kerry among non-Jews, and living outside the Northeast and in suburbs or rural localities, which diminished support for Kerry. Education, too, acts differently on non-Jews than on Jews. Completion of high school or having several years of college corresponds negatively to Democratic political orientation. If so, the main residual similarities between Jews and non-Jews are the positive relation between academic education and voting for Kerry and the negative links between the factors of religious identification and support of this presidential candidate. Notably, the relations of gender (positive), marital status of being single or divorced (positive), and income (negative) behave similarly among Jews and non-Jews, but are statistically significant only among the latter. Taken together, the independent variables are much less effective in explaining differences in non-Jews' voting patterns: the explained variance of 13.7 percent is less than half the level for Jews. The inference is that non-Jews' political preferences are abetted by other factors that were not indexed by the data used in this study. These factors may operate at the individual level, but others may relate to the American social, economic, and political situation at the macro level. It would seem that Jews, perhaps due to their minority status, are guided first and foremost by individual and group considerations and only to a secondary degree by general circumstances.

Even when Jews and non-Jews resemble each other in sociodemographic traits and religious identification, they diverge in their political preferences. Jews were twice as likely to vote for Kerry as non-Jews. This preference was even more salient when compared with the voting of mainline Protestants. However, according to the size of the coefficients in the last column, black Protestants, Muslims, and adherents of other faiths were even more likely to vote for Kerry than Jews were. When mainline Protestants were set as the reference category, most groups tended to support the Democratic candidate more than the Republican. The exceptions were Mormons and evangelical Protestants, who were less in favor of Kerry, i.e., clearly preferred his rival, Bush. Both the significance of group belonging and the increase in explained variance in the last model relative to the previous one (from 14.1 percent to 23.4 percent) attest to the importance of religious group considerations in Americans' political voting patterns.

Historical review and more recent observations show clearly that, despite mild fluctuations, American Jews tend to be Democrats. Their massive majority turnout for the Democratic presidential candidate in 2004, John Kerry, contrasts sharply with non-Jews' small majority preference for the Republican candidate, George W. Bush. Comparison of Jews with other specific religious groups reveals a similarity with black Protestants, Muslims, adherents of other faiths, and the unaffiliated, all of whom lent majority support to Kerry. According to the 2013 Pew survey of American Jews, this inclination to the Democratic Party continued well into the second decade of the twenty-first century. It revealed that 70 percent of Jews identified with or leaned toward the Democratic Party, as against 22 percent who favored the Republican Party, whereas 8 percent either preferred an independent candidate or had no preference at all.

Affiliation with a religious group is a significant determinant of voting behavior. Distinguishing between Jews and non-Jews, as well as by specific religious affiliation, yielded strong and

TABLE 5.3 DIRECTION (> 1 POSITIVE, < 1 NEGA-
TIVE) AND MAGNITUDE OF EFFECTS OF SOCIODE-
MOGRAPHIC CHARACTERISTICS, RELIGIOUS IDEN-
TIFICATION, AND GROUP AFFILIATION ON VOTING
PATTERNS, UNITED STATES, 2007

	Jews	Non-Jews	Total with group belonging	Total with religious identity
Age 18–29	0.878	1.334***	1.315***	1.207***
Age 30–44	0.285***	1.122***	1.091*	1.016
Age 45–64	0.663	1.177***	1.162***	1.095**
Female	1.294	1.391***	1.387***	1.388***
Midwest	1.782*	1.013	1.035	1.121***
South	1.649*	0.790***	0.811***	0.823***
West	2.279***	0.759***	0.782***	0.894***
Suburban	1.536*	0.615***	0.631***	0.709***
Rural	1.307	0.514**	0.522***	0.643***
Foreign-born	0.251***	1.638***	1.521***	1.331***
Single	1.258	1.973***	1.957***	1.688***
Divorced/ separated	1.317	1.126***	1.131***	1.061
Widowed	1.385	1.053	1.061	1.032
Intermarried	0.833	1.069	1.068	1.077*
High school graduate	1.905	0.863***	0.868***	0.888**
Some college	3.248*	0.890**	0.900*	0.919
College graduate	7.776***	1.186***	1.211***	1.229***
Medium income	0.979	0.836***	0.839***	0.842***
High income	0.632	0.688***	0.687***	0.725***
Very high income	0.764	0.611***	0.615***	0.640***
Importance of religion	0.582***	0.752***	0.750***	0.803***

(*continued*)

(*continued*)

	Jews	Non-Jews	Total with group belonging	Total with religious identity
Attendance at religious services	0.791**	0.846***	0.845***	0.870***
Jews	-	-	2.026***	2.541***
Evangelical Protestants	-	-	-	0.635***
Black Protestants	-	-	-	8.393***
Catholics	-	-	-	1.215***
Mormons	-	-	-	0.415***
Other Christians	-	-	-	1.753***
Muslims	-	-	-	7.360***
Other faiths	-	-	-	4.340***
Unaffiliated				1.711***
% variance explained (R^2)	29.0%	13.7%	14.1%	23.4%

significant effects. These findings support the sociological model of individuals' political behavior. They emphasize the importance that Americans attribute to their religious identity and the role that it plays in the ultimate civic ritual, voting for president. Still, religious groups differ in the extent of their readiness to engage religion with politics (judged by the size of the coefficient). A comparative view of all ten religious groups shows that Jews exhibit a fairly high level of such relations. The findings for Jews and non-Jews alike lend empirical support to the hypothesis that associates religiosity, in both attitude and behavior, with political patterns (while stronger religious identification inhibits a democratic orientation). Hence the various religious groups in the United States are deployed along the political spectrum in ways that also indicate the significance of their religious convictions and behaviors. Slightly less clear are the relations between socioeconomic status, reflected particularly in income, and political preferences, which were insignificant among Jews and meaningful among non-Jews. Consistent with the rational-choice model, Jews may be less inclined to view political behavior as something that should benefit them at the individual level, whereas for non-Jews this is an important consideration. Furthermore, Jewish exogamy per se, as opposed to endogamy, erodes voting for the Democratic candidate. In this sense, intermarried Jews distance themselves somewhat from traditional Jewish political orientations in favor of non-Jewish patterns. The effect of intermarriage on voting, however, is not strong. That intermarried Jews deviate from the traditional Jewish political leaning toward Democrats somewhat refutes the theory of early-life political socialization (the "psychological" perspective); that is, being born and raised in a Jewish family does not have lasting effects in terms of political identification, which somewhat fade after intermarriage.

Indeed, until the latter decades of the twentieth century, elite opinion held that ethnicity ought not be a factor in American politics. Americans, it was asserted, should be politically active and vote on the basis of America's best interest, or that of the larger community, and not on the basis of narrow and insular ethnic interests.[1] In reality, however, ethnicity has long played an important role in American politics. Politicians are well aware of this; "balancing the ticket" is only one of the most prominent manifestations of it. Although such involvement varies among groups, as Thomas Sowell (1981) pointed out, the findings of the Pew survey show that, insofar as religion is concerned, group belonging is a paramount determinant of political behavior in early twenty-first-century America.

EPILOGUE

Jews and the American Religious Landscape

THE SUBFIELD OF SOCIOLOGY
OF RELIGION

B Y SOCIOLOGICAL definition, a religion is a set of beliefs and practices that relates to sacred elements and binds people into social groups (Durkheim 1995 [1912]). An important role of a religion is the promotion of uniformity and solidarity among group members and opportunities to express shared norms and tasks (Berger 1967). Religion also enhances stability and social stratification by sacralizing norms and values (Roberts 1990). This perspective underscores the social and cultural function of religion. Religion, however, also provides meaning in life and conveys a sense of identity and belonging (Weber 1978 [1922]). It sets forth a worldview that relates to nature, the self, society, and the cosmos (Geertz 1973; Roberts 1990). Religion has a dimension of content that turns it into a set of responses to existential human dilemmas (Weber 1978 [1922]). From this perspective, religion is mainly something that provides the individual with utility (Roberts 1990). Be their role social or individual, religion and faith in a deity guide people in how to behave and, accordingly, create ethical considerations

(Swatos and Gustafson 1992). The functionality of religion within a social reality transforms religion into a universal culture (Berger 1967). Obviously, however, the functions that religion fulfills and its modus operandi vary widely between religions or religious groups; otherwise, religions would be of no sociological interest (Christiano, Swatos, and Kivisto 2008).

Religious patterns, like all social phenomena, should be examined from a comparative point of view (Wuthnow 2003). A systematic search for similarities and dissimilarities is anchored in the perspective of comparative sociology (Marsh 1966) and is helpful in reaching broadly valid conclusions. Comparative analysis of macro or micro factors of religion, or of relations between religion and social variables, may be performed across groups, times, or places (Rebhun 2011). In view of the very large number of religious groups, social scientists often merge significantly similar ones into sects, denominations, or churches. Although such a construction of the data has its drawbacks, it is unavoidable as an analytic tool and draws on the tracing of the historical origins of groups, the reading of their religious texts, and scientific observations over the years (Roberts 1990). The indicators chosen for the assessment of similarities or dissimilarities among such groups must, of course, be truly comparable. Still, one must realize that a given behavior by adherents of a defined religion or culture may acquire different meanings or degrees of importance in accordance with its specific religious idea, value, and doctrinal system. Furthermore, items presented in a closed-ended questionnaire leave respondents no wiggle room for the articulation of alternative forms of religiosity. Hence negative answers to certain questions do not necessarily indicate that one respondent is less religious or less orthodox than another (Roberts 1990). There may be patterns that are specific to and of major importance for a given faith, but they will not receive any attention in a general study that limits itself to the investigation of patterns that are relevant to all religions.

Another important characteristic of research into the sociology of religion is its interdisciplinary nature (Wuthnow 2003). The sociology of religion, as a specific subfield of sociology, has a defined intellectual tradition and defined issues of interest such as religious denominations, community profiles, and religious beliefs and practices. Religious patterns, however, are also related, either as causes or as effects, to other facets of social life including demography, economics, and politics. While each such discipline has theories of its own, all are amenable to multivariate design and similar quantitative approaches, hence they encourage a multidimensional evaluation of the religious factors. Such a comprehensive approach is essential and rests on the view that modern society is not synonymous with secularism and that, despite social and personal tendencies brought on by the development of civilization, the phenomenon of religion has retained much vitality (Bellah et al. 1996 [1985]; Brown 1992).

One prerequisite for the application of research on the sociology of religion in a manner that would remain true to the comprehensive notion of intergroup comparison and interdisciplinarianism is an empirical infrastructure. In the case of the United States, insofar as quantitative data are concerned, this task is anything but easy because official surveys cannot ask about matters of creed due to the separation of religion and state. A single exception was a Current Population Survey from 1957, carried out by the U.S. Census Bureau among thirty-five thousand households, which included an item about religious identity. Indeed, the survey yielded estimates of the size of religious groups and insights about some of their characteristics. However, it was limited to demographic and socioeconomic patterns and took no interest whatsoever in religious or political ones. Research centers and other private entities, such as the General Social Survey or Gallup, often collect data that reveal respondents' religious affiliation but do not investigate enough cases to adequately analyze small religious groups. This drawback is overcome in the present study with the help of the large nationwide and representative survey undertaken by the Pew Forum in 2007.

One religious group of this type, small but nevertheless central to understanding America, is the Jews. The corpus of social scientific knowledge about Jews' is rich in analyses that focus largely on this target population only, relative to one point in time (e.g., Goldstein and Goldstein 1996; Hartman and Hartman 1996; Phillips and Fishman 2006; Waxman 2001), in an attempt to track changes in a specific topic over time (e.g., Rebhun 2004) or to compare Jews in different parts of the country (e.g., Hartman and Sheskin 2012). Insofar as Jews were compared with non-Jews through the integrated use of nationwide Jewish population surveys and census data, respectively, non-Jews were introduced as a homogeneous group, ruling out specificity in religious affiliations (e.g., Chiswick 2007; Hartman and Hartman 2009; Rebhun 1997a). These studies emphasize the profound controversy that exists among researchers over the nature and manifestations of Jewish existence in American society. At the core of the debate are estimates of the number of Jews in the U.S. and attacks on methods that scholars adopted to arrive at them (DellaPergola 2014a; Dutwin, Ben Porath, and Miller 2014; Saxe, Sasson, and Aronson 2014). In fact, even recently, when the initial findings of the 2013 Pew survey of the Jewish population were released, different views emerged about whom to include in the enumeration of Jews. Should only self-defined Jews be counted, or should the reckoning also cover people who are Jewish and something else (the "partial Jews")? (DellaPergola 2013b; Pew Research Center 2013; Saxe 2013). No less salient are the disagreements over the choice of indicators for the assessment of Jewish vitality and the weight given to each indicator (Cohen 1983; Goldstein and Goldstein 1996; Rebhun 2011). Yet another aspect of the issue is the method of measurement and, in particular, whether the patterns revealed among the younger generation will accompany them throughout time or change, particularly in the direction of gaining strength, as youth enter into more advanced stages of the life cycle such as that of family formation (DellaPergola 1992; Goldscheider 2004). Accordingly, various conclusions have been proposed with regard to the trajectories on which American Jewry is marching: assimilation (to the extent of disappearance), the continuation of their presence and group commitment, or the adjustment to existential realities of twenty-first-century American society in ways that do not involve religious or ethnic disconnection. The foregoing analysis and evaluation in comparison with other religious groups cast American Jews in an unfamiliar new light.

NUMBERS MATTER

The number of Jews in America has been stable and has even grown slightly in the past four decades: from 5.4 million in 1970 to 5.5 million in 1990 and 5.7 million at around the end of the first decade of the twenty-first century. This stability is the result of a dynamic of factors that determine population size, which sometimes operate in opposing directions that cancel each other out. The set of factors includes, on the downward side, "actual

Jewish fertility" (the number of children per Jewish woman
who grow up and identify as Jews), which is under the intergenerational replacement level and is causing the aging of the
population and, ultimately, a surplus of deaths over births. On
the upward side, American Jews have been gaining from religious accession and international migration. Another factor that
should be taken into account is the echo effect of the baby boom,
namely the entrance in recent years of large numbers of grand-
children of those born after World War II into critical stages of
family formation and childbearing. Even if each grandchild has
only one child or two children, collectively they will produce a
new and relatively large cohort of Jewish children. Notably, too,
although interfaith marriage is more common among Jewish
men than among Jewish women, gender differences in exogamy
rates have narrowed among later marriage cohorts. That the
mother is Jewish increases the likelihood that her children will
be raised and educated as Jews, pushing up actual Jewish fertility. More generally, the ascendancy of pluralism and multicul-
turalism in the United States encourages individuals to express
group belonging, including those of mixed parentage who may
have been raised without a religious identity and now choose to
declare their Jewishness.

While the number of Jews has been more or less constant,
the total American population has grown. By implication, the
share of Jews and, in turn, their social and political strength have
fallen. Furthermore, today's American Jews are operating in an
American society that is undergoing far-reaching changes in its
religious composition. The share of Protestants has diminished,
and most adherents of this faith no longer belong to the mainline denominations that most closely resemble Jews in their social
and political patterns; rather, evangelical Protestants have risen

to the fore. Conversely, the share of those who affirm no religious belonging whatsoever has been growing robustly. In other words, the extremes of the American religious continuum—the very religious and the very secular—are thickening, while those of the middle, the segment that best suits most Jews (who are Conservative or Reform), are losing ground. Since religion figures significantly in shaping the image of American society, it is developing in directions that may be less sympathetic to and comfortable for many Jews.

The Jewish population is also experiencing trends of diffusion of religious identity, as two groups record proportional increases: the Orthodox, on the one hand, and those who consider themselves Jewish but do not view Judaism as a religion, on the other (Ament 2005). While the former maintain the ramparts of religious and social separatism from non-Jews, their ethnic Jewish peers (with no religion) are lowering the barriers that distinguish them from the rest of America. This process is gathering additional momentum because in the United States today, largely due to the influx of immigrants from the Far East, there are religious confessions that are not Judeo-Christian whose membership is growing vigorously; collectively, they already outnumber the Jews and are poised to continue increasing. Their high educational and economic attainments make them appropriate marriage partners for Jews (Kim and Leavitt 2012), causing Judaism to mingle with nonmonotheistic religious patterns.

Despite their small numbers, American Jews have contributed much to America's greatness (Lipset and Raab 1995). This is mainly attributed to the uniquely welcoming American environment and the Jews' concentration on the upper rungs of the social ladder and professional echelons in politics, the economy, academia, and the media—all supported by the liberal values that Jews and the WASP mainstream share. The proportional decline of the Jewish population, the changes in the religious composition of the American population and, accordingly, its social and cultural patterns, along with the ongoing shift of the color line in the direction of greater equilibrium between whites and nonwhites (the latter group including Hispanics), may weaken the commonality of Jews and the majority population, with similar outcomes on the impact of the Jews' imprint on American society.

INSIGHTS FROM THE MICRO

Judging by their individual characteristics, American Jews enjoy higher education and income than any other religious group. Concurrently, they have one of the highest rates of intermarriage and one of the lowest levels of religious identification, second only to Americans who profess no religious affiliation. If, in the past, Jews were concerned about their social and economic integration, today they mainly face challenges of communal cohesion and assuring the group commitment of their successors.

At the heart of this study was an attempt to assess the role of religious affiliation as a determinant of patterns in various important areas of life. The analysis was constructed stage by stage, adding a phenomenon investigated at an early stage to the explanatory factors behind a new phenomenon in the next stage. As figure E.1 shows, religious belonging (together with selected individual sociodemographic characteristics) was introduced for the evaluation of differences in education and income attainments (stage 1). Thereafter, education and income were held constant for the assessment of relations between religion and marriage patterns within or out of the faith (stage B). Then, marital composition became a determinant of the strength of religious identification (stage C). Finally, all these factors together were inserted into a model that yielded an insight into the specific political leanings of each religious group (stage D). Admittedly, the data used are not longitudinal in the sense that they can detect causality, i.e., show that a characteristic attained in an early stage of life evolved into another characteristic and so on. Nevertheless, the religious identity of many individuals is the one into which they were born, if not one they adopted with certainty in an early stage of the life cycle, thus allowing it to influence the other behavioral patterns that this study investigated. Likewise, education and other structural characteristics of economy and geography steer people through a socialization process to the norms and values of society in general and their group of religious belonging in particular. It stands to reason that all these, in turn, are more formative in, rather than influenced by, political orientation.

Throughout this interweaving of traits, which begins with the single factor of Jewish versus non-Jewish religious affiliation (followed by a distinction among non-Jews by specific denominations) and picks up additional factors along the way until the chain is complete, religion proves to be significant

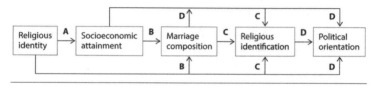

FIGURE E.1. TESTING FRAMEWORK OF THE ROLE OF RELIGIOUS
AFFILIATION IN MAJOR AREAS OF LIFE

in major areas of life. The strength of religion in social, identificational, and political patterns is evident in all American denominations. However, it often acts in different
directions and rhythms in each denomination, casting the
denominations into different hierarchies in various domains.
As it does so, similarities and dissimilarities among religious
groups come into view. Following the testing framework of
the investigation, it is found that being Jewish, as opposed to
being non-Jewish, enhances the tendency to higher education and income, mitigates the proclivity to religious exogamy, reinforces religious identification, and corresponds to
Democratic political leanings. Jewish affiliation versus non-
Jewish affiliation is related to social attainment, religious group
commitment, and egalitarian, pluralistic, and tolerant worldviews. The religious group belonging of Jews does not impede,
but rather encourages—in a manner most appropriate to the
American ethos—the structural incorporation of a minority
that retains its particularistic patterns without challenge and
embraces American democracy at the same time.

The differences between Jews and non-Jews are strongly
affected by patterns of specific groups among the latter (table
6.1). Still, being Jewish amplifies educational and economic
attainments more powerfully than affiliation with any other
religious group does. Furthermore, Jews are no different from
mainline Protestants, who were long the archetype toward
which other groups were expected to converge, in their predis-
position to marry out of the faith. Also, even though Jews rank
low among religious groups in the hierarchy of religious identification, they are very close to the reference group, mainline
Protestants. The same may be said about their political orientation. That Jews occupy a low rung on the religious identificational

TABLE E.1 HIERARCHY OF RELIGIOUS AFFILIATION FOR SOCIOECONOMIC ATTAINMENT, INTERFAITH MARRIAGE, RELIGIOUS IDENTIFICATION, AND POLITICAL (DEMOCRATIC) ORIENTATION

Education	Earnings	Interfaith marriage	Democratic orientation
Jews	Jews	Other faiths	Black Protestants
Muslims	Mainline Protestants	Other Christians	Muslims
Other faiths	Catholics	Jews	Other faiths
Mainline Protestants	Other Christians	Muslims	
Mormons	Other faiths	Mainline Protestants	
Other Christians	Unaffiliated	Catholics	
Unaffiliated	Evangelical Protestants	Evangelical Protestants	
Catholics	Muslims	Black Protestants	
Evangelical Protestants	Mormons	Mormons	
Black Protestants	Black Protestants		

Interpersonal identification	Personal identification	Impersonal identification
Evangelical Protestants	Evangelical Protestants	Evangelical Protestants
Black Protestants	Mormons	Black Protestants
Mormons	Black Protestants	Mormons

(continued)

(continued)

Interpersonal identification	Personal identification	Impersonal identification	Democratic orientation
Other Christians	Catholics	Other Christians	Jews
Muslims	Muslims	Muslims	Other Christians
Mainline Protestants	Mainline Protestants	Mainline Protestants	Unaffiliated
Catholics	Other Christians	Catholics	Catholics
Other faiths	Other faiths	Jews	Mainline Protestants
Jews	Jews	Other faiths	Evangelical Protestants
Unaffiliated	Unaffiliated	Unaffiliated	Mormons

The order is based on the direction and size of coefficients in the respective multivariate analyses.

ladder is mainly due to the strong religious convictions of evangelical Protestants, black Protestants, Mormons, and Muslims. Their low ranking on the identification scale, sometimes brushing against the religiously unaffiliated, should not be misconstrued: in terms of the strength of their relations with religious identification, Jews are much closer to mainline Protestants than to the unaffiliated. Overall, while concentrating at the highest socioeconomic levels, American Jews swim in the traditional and institutional American mainstream and do not veer toward the extremes.

Alongside the unique role of Jewish religious affiliation as against non-Jewish, the other factors in the array of this inquiry also, at times, react to each other in different ways among each of the population groups. In particular, Jews' educational attainments do not correlate with any form of assimilation. Higher education has no significant relation to Jews' interfaith marriage and, for the most part, does not dampen Jews' religious identification. The opposite is true for non-Jews: higher education encourages marital heterogeneity and weakens cognitive religious identification both personal and impersonal. Another parameter of attainment, high income, weakens religious identification among Jews and non-Jews alike. Interfaith marriage mitigates the interpersonal and impersonal religious identification of Jews and non-Jews, but does not undermine religious faith. Likewise, the effects of education (positive), income (negative), interfaith marriage (not significant), and religious identification (negative) on political orientation are similar among both population groups. Contemplating Jewish affiliation and Jews' attainments together, one may state that early twenty-first-century America allows Jews to maintain their particularistic identity, attain socioeconomic prosperity, and be confident that neither condition will harm their religious vitality and continuity.

Yet there are other individual factors that consistently weaken Jews' group connections. The first is age. Young generations of Jews are more inclined to marry outside the faith than their parents were, even if they resemble their parents in other sociodemographic affinities. A second factor is the geographic space in which Jews choose to live. In a departure from the past (until the middle of the previous century), when most Jews congregated in the Northeast and lived close to each other in urban centers, in recent decades they have been moving to the West and the South and, at the local level, to the suburbs. Consequently, the Jewish population is more scattered and physically distant from communal institutions and services than before. Life in these areas is associated with a tendency to interfaith marriage and lower levels of religious identification. A third conspicuous determinant of weak identification is marital status. Not only mixed marriage but also being unmarried (i.e., single, divorced/separated, or widowed), a status that defines more than half of adult Jews in the United States today, distances the individual from religious behaviors and beliefs. Furthermore, Jewish immigrants exhibit a weaker religious identification than their American-born peers. A large share of this group is composed of former Soviet Jews who had spent decades living in a country that repressed all religious conviction. That they chose to settle in the United States and not in Israel attests to their loose connection with Judaism. What is more, many Israelis who moved to the United States are not religious; they find local Jews' community patterns foreign and often avoid involvement in organized Jewish activities.

THE MESO AND MACRO SPHERES: SPECULATIONS AND IMPLICATIONS FOR RESEARCH

Contemplating religion through the prism of the individual (the micro level) proved rather effective in understanding socioeconomic attainments, religious identification, and political preferences. A large amount of the differences in these behaviors, however, remains unexplained; it probably traces to individual characteristics that are not documented in the data and, no less important, to the large units of analysis—the local religious community (the meso level) and American society at large (the macro level). In fact, the individual factors of geography, family, nativity status, and age, which have a major effect on religious patterns, do not operate in a vacuum; instead, they hint at the effects of the other two spheres. Obviously, any discussion of community and national factors should be treated as speculation or as informed guesswork at most.

Localism is the actual focus of activity in an ethnoreligious community. Alternatively expressed, the combination of historical, structural, and institutional variables that jointly create ethnoreligious communities includes what may be defined as a local factor (Lazerwitz 1977). People who share religious and normative views, communal institutions, and the fundamental cohesive presence of coreligionists create together a convenient environment and meaningful local characteristics. The individual's religious and ethnic behavior is strongly anchored in experiences within his or her immediate environment, with local people and in defined contexts.

Jewish immigrants in the United States in the late nineteenth/ early twentieth centuries were characterized by the model of the *landsmanshaft*, i.e., living in a limited number of streets and neighborhoods according to town of origin abroad. This was an especially extreme expression of physical segregation and strong ties among Jews and between them and communal institutions. The geographic patterns of preference for suburbs and Sunbelt regions thrust Jews into an encounter with a diffuse communal infrastructure and limited access to religious and cultural services and activities. It is the nature of suburbs to sprawl over a large area, situating people at distances from each other and from their institutions (Rebhun 1995). To surmount the obstacle of the physical distance, people must make an effort to stay in touch with one another and to participate intensively in formal settings such as parochial schools or houses of worship as well as informal ones such as social networks (Goldstein 1981, 1991). Moreover, some large institutions and activities cannot replicate themselves across a welter of suburbs in a metropolitan area; they will locate themselves in the center of the city, creating a further encumbrance for their users. The American South and West are also relatively new in terms of Jewish settlement. Their Jewish community infrastructures are not yet well developed and supple. Moreover, many Jews who live in these regions moved to them from the veteran regions of settlement, the Northeast and the Midwest (Goldstein and Goldstein 1996; Rebhun 2002). It is known that internal migration can disrupt communal relations and religious identification (Finke 1989; Welch and Baltzell 1984). As far as the South is concerned, many Jews, especially the elderly, divide their time seasonally between that region and another home in a different region (dual residence; Rebhun and Goldstein 2006), routinely shaking the structure of the local community and its services.

One possible substitute for the official institutional setting is advanced (read: cyber) technology. Its embrace would transfer the Jewish connection from the public domain to the private one where people can express their identity at the times and intensities that are convenient for them. The modalities of such expression include, among others, participation in social utilities (e.g., Facebook and Twitter) comprised of other Jews or discussion groups on Jewish matters; remote online Jewish learning for both children and adults as a surrogate for schools and face-to-face gatherings; dating through websites; Jewish philanthropy by electronic transfer of payment; and virtual visits to Jewish museums and sites. The physical community of tangibly accessible peers and institutions can be replaced today by a virtual community that communicates, educates itself, and consumes culture electronically. The former type of community appears to be more visible and effective than the latter for social cohesion and religious and ethnic vitality, but the electronic methods offer many opportunities that suit present-day preferred forms of socialization and religious orientations that are meaningful for the individual's group belonging. This reality is amplified by the Jewish presence on the Internet, which far exceeds its proportion in the total American (and world) population, and by Jews' intensive usage of it, presumably due to their high educational attainment (Sheskin and Liben 2015).

To empirically estimate the effects of Jewish population density and supply of community institutions and services on individuals' religious patterns, one must use community surveys and combine their data with contextual indicators. Indeed, the regional differences among Jews that were found in this study suggest that local communities, particularly those in the suburbs and in the Southern and Western states, should perform a reassessment and seek new ways to attract their Jewish inhabitants to organized Jewish life. Nevertheless, the meso unit of analysis—the local community—should incorporate religious patterns that are acquired online. Although such forms are measured at the individual level, many of them are synonymous with the role that was traditionally embodied at the communal level or even at the national (or global) one. Such an approach, of course, should be adopted as well for the assessment of the religious identification of members of other faiths.

American Jews have deployed across all fifty states and the District of Columbia. Several characteristics of the population composition and general socioeconomic conditions of each state may help to understand variations in religious patterns. While some of these factors affect all religious minorities similarly, others will be of consequence mainly for their Jewish inhabitants. One contextual line of argument views minorities as largely conforming to the patterns of the host environment. If so, the more religious a destination state is, the more members of religious minorities may bolster their own religious identification while tailoring their rituals and worship styles to those of the majority population. Another contextual factor is the political orientation of the local population—liberal or conservative—as reflected in its voting behavior. The coloring of a state as "blue" attests to the presence there of a large number of people who are characterized by a strong tolerance of minorities, which, for that reason, may become more confident expressing religious difference. The more heterogeneous a state is, i.e., the more its population accommodates many religious minorities, each with its own religious patterns, the more Jews will seek to maintain their particularistic group identification. In this regard, it should be noted that some minorities, specifically African Americans and Muslims, hold rather strong anti-Jewish prejudices and sentiments; a large concentration of them in a given state may encourage different types of anti-Jewish manifestations that may either inhibit Jews from displaying religioethnic singularities, especially public ones, or prompt them to combat the anti-Semitism, resulting in greater communal involvement and cohesion. A major macro factor that elicits accusations against Jews in various places and times is the worsening of economic conditions. Such reactions reflect the view that Jews hold key economic positions and wield excessive power. A paramount economic factor in this respect is the unemployment rate; the higher the unemployment rate in a given state, the more it provokes expressions against and stereotyping of Jews, with the possibility of either weakening or strengthening religioethnic identification.

Another macrolevel dimension is the period of socialization and exposure to processes and events that characterize American society. This includes, in particular, the broadening of religious diversity and pluralism, the growing incidence of lack of religious belonging, and some vitiation of traditional religious patterns. It is possible that some of the religious beliefs and behaviors that all faiths share, those at the core of this analysis, are being replaced by, or marginalized relative to, particularistic patterns within each religion. In the context of American Jews, these beliefs and behaviors include, but are not confined to, Holocaust remembrance, concern for needy Jews in other countries, and attachment to Israel.

In fact, the macro unit of analysis may extend beyond the borders of the United States. The Jews have a homeland, Israel. Whether they regard it as a religious, spiritual, or ancestral homeland, events there may affect the rhythm of individual and collective identification in America. It is known especially that the religioethnic identification of members of a diaspora gathers strength at times of unrest overseas (Jacobson 2002); in the case of American Jews, this phenomenon occurs occasionally in regard to the long and as yet unresolved conflict in the Middle East. At times, decisions made in faraway Israel, such as those relating to improvements of or infringements on the status of the non-Orthodox movements there, may affect the identificational patterns of Diaspora Jews, foremost those in America, where the progressive denominations are widespread. Hence, religioethnic identification is fluid and may change from time to time.

A FINAL REMARK

The main purpose of this book is to offer a new perspective on contemporary American Jewry. Just the same, its dozens of detailed figures and tables may present readers who are interested in other religious groups with a great wealth of data. Furthermore, the insights arising from an investigation of Jews should be important for expectations pertaining to other religious minority groups. As previous studies have suggested, Jews have often been ahead of other religious or ethnic minorities of European descent in challenging the demographic and sociocultural opportunities of the majority population (Goldstein 1969). But also for new minority groups of recent immigrants, before trying to assess their integration prospects one should examine the path taken by previous groups in depth. Only then can the elements of continuity and disjuncture that exist between the experience of past immigrant groups and those of the present day be properly evaluated (Alba and Nee 2003). Accordingly, while this study highlighted Jews from a broad comparative perspective, other religious groups may avail themselves of the Jewish case to attain a better understanding of themseles.

APPENDIX A1

Religious Identificational Variables

Used in Analysis

1. Should churches and other houses of worship keep out of political matters—or should they express their views on day-to-day social and political questions? [RELPOL]

    1-keep out; 2-should express views.

2. Evolution is the best explanation for the origins of human life on earth: [EVOLHUM]

    1-completely agree; 2-mostly agree; 3-mostly disagree; 4-completely disagree.

3. When it comes to questions of right and wrong, to which do you look most for guidance? [RIGWRN]

    1-philosophy and reason; 2-scientific information (regrouped into one category); 3-practical experience and common sense; 4-religious teaching and beliefs.

4. Aside from weddings and funerals, how often do you attend religious services: [RELSERV]

    1-never; 2-seldom; 3-a few times a year; 4-once or twice a month; 5-once a week; 6-more than once a week.

5. How important is religion in your life? [IMPREL]
> 1-not at all important; 2-not too important; 3-somewhat important; 4-very important.

6. Thinking about the church or house of worship where you attend religious services most often, how often do you participate in a choir or other musical program there? [CHOIR]
> 1-never (including those who never or seldom attend religious services in Q 4); 2-seldom; 3-several times a year; 4-once or twice a month; 5-at least once a week.

7. Thinking about the church or house of worship where you attend religious services most often, how often do you do community volunteer work through your place of worship? [COMVOL]
> 1-never (including those who never or seldom attend religious services in Q. 4); 2-seldom; 3-several times a year; 4-once or twice a month; 5-at least once a week.

8. Thinking about the church or house of worship where you attend religious services most often, how often do you work with children or youth there? [CHILD]
> 1-never (including those who never or seldom attend religious services in Q. 4); 2-seldom; 3-several times a year; 4-once or twice a month; 5-at least once a week.

9. Thinking about the church or house of worship where you attend religious services most often, how often do you participate in social activities, such as meals, club meetings, or other gatherings there? [SOCACT]
> 1-never (including those who never or seldom attend religious services in Q. 4); 2-seldom; 3-several times a year; 4-once or twice a month; 5-at least once a week.

10. Are you or your family official members of a local church or house of worship? [MEMBER]

    1-no; 2-yes.

11. Do you believe in God or a universal spirit? [those who believe in God were further asked] How certain are you about this belief? [BELV]

    1-no (don't believe in God); 2-yes, not at all certain; 3-yes, not too certain; 4-yes, fairly certain; 5-yes, absolutely certain.

12. What comes closest to your view of God? [VIEWGOD]

    1-God is an impersonal force; 2-God is a person.

13. Do you believe in life after death? [LIFDET]

    1-no; 2-yes.

14. Do you think there is a heaven, where people who have led good lives are eternally rewarded? [HEAV]

    1-no; 2-yes.

15. Which comes closest to your view; the Bible/Torah/Koran/Holy Scripture [HOLYBK]

    1-is a book written by men and is not the word of God; 2-is the word of God.

16. Outside of attending religious services, do you pray: [PRAY]

    1-never; 2-seldom;3-a few times a month; 4-once a week; 5-a few times a week; 6. once a day; 7-several times a day.

17. How often do you participate in prayer groups, Scripture study groups, or religious education programs? [PRAYGRP]

    1-never; 2-seldom; 3-several times a year; 4-once or twice a month; 5-at least once a week.

18. How often do you read Scripture outside of religious services? [READSCRPT]

> 1-never; 2-seldom; 3-several times a year; 4-once or twice a month; 5-at least once a week.

APPENDIX A2

Loading of Questions on Religious Identification Factors: Principle Component Varimax Rotation

Factor	Loading on Factor
Factor I. Interpersonal	
Participation in social activities (SOCACT)	.816
Community volunteer work (COMVOL)	.814
Work with children (CHILD)	.763
Religious services (RELSERV)	.719
Participation in prayer group (PRAYGRP)	.696
Participation in a choir (CHOIR)	.632
Read scripture (READSCRPT)	.519
Membership in house of worship (MEMBER)	.503
Factor II. Personal	
Believe in heaven (HEAV)	.783
Believe in God (BELV)	.780
Believe life after death (LIFDET)	.737
Importance of religion (IMPREL)	.618
Private pray (PRAY)	.582
View of God (VIEWGOD)	.542
View of Bible/Holy Scripture (HOLYBK)	.522

(continued)

(continued)

Factor III. Impersonal

Guidance for right and wrong (RIGWRN)	.692
Origin of human life (EVOLHUM)	.691
Political matters (RELPOL)	.540

NOTES

I. POPULATION SIZE AND DYNAMICS

1. Notably, the American Religious Identification Survey (ARIS) of 2001, which covered a large random sample of adults in various American religious groups, yielded a similar estimate of the number of Jews (5.3 million; Kosmin and Keysar 2006).

2. The share of "ethnic" Jews is somewhat lower than that produced by many recent surveys of American Jewry. These national surveys estimate their share at one Jew in five. The Pew survey omits, among other things, persons of non-Jewish origin who married Jews and became Jews without converting as well as converts who expressed no religious identity when interviewed for the survey.

3. Notably, ARIS set the share of children under age eighteen at 24 percent (Mayer, Kosmin, and Keysar 2002). Application of this proportion of children to the findings in the Pew survey would bring the core Jewish population in 2007 to six million.

4. Even though the total estimate in this study, derived from the 2007 Pew survey, closely approximates that of the 2103 survey, the former may be slightly biased toward that segment of the Jewish population that considers their Jewishness a religion.

5. The Pew team gathered verbatim responses (Saxe, Sasson, and Krasner Aronson 2014); these materials may also be helpful in assigning interviewees to the Jewish or some other population.

6. This group does not include religiously unaffiliated persons who were raised as Jews; they constitute part of the Jewish group. Since this study centers on Jews, it was decided that this would allow the discussion to adhere strongly to the definition of the "core" Jewish population as is common in the social science literature; thus it would facilitate a full estimation of the size and characteristics of this population. However, other respondents who professed no religion were incorporated into one distinct group of the "unaffiliated." This group, composed of a hodgepodge of people of diverse religious backgrounds, has been steadily growing in recent years and should be given separate treatment in the investigation of American social and cultural patterns.

7. The 2013 Pew survey of the American Jewish population estimated the average number of children ever born per Jewish adult aged forty to fifty at 1.9 and found differences between Jews by religion (2.1) and ethnic Jews (1.5). The estimate of completed Jewish fertility in the current study, 2.1, may actually be higher because the weight of Jews by religion was higher in the 2007 Pew survey than in the 2013 survey.

8. These differences are supported by other studies that set the total fertility of all American Christians at 2.3, of Muslims at 2.5, and of Jews at 1.9 (Pew Research Center 2011, 2013).

9. The number of foreign-born Americans increased from around ten million in 1970 to twenty million in 1990 and doubled again, to nearly forty million, by 2010 (http://www.census.gov.how/infographics/foreign_born html). For estimates of Jewish immigration to the United States, see DellaPergola 2013a).

10. The survey questions about upbringing faith are not as detailed as those about current religion and do not allow full differentiation among those raised as evangelical, mainline, or black Protestants. Therefore, all Protestants are aggregated here as members of one group.

11. The age distribution of the Jewish population was calculated with the youngest taken into account. The results of this calculation are as follows: zero to seventeen—19.5 percent; eighteen to twenty-nine—17.1 percent; thirty to forty-four—16.5 percent; forty-five to sixty-four—29.5 percent; sixty-five and over—17.4 percent.

2. SPATIAL AND SOCIOECONOMIC STRATIFICATION

1. Notably, among those aged sixty-five plus, the share of degree holders among Muslims is higher than among Jews. This finding, however, should be treated cautiously due to the very small number of Muslim respondents in this age group.

2. Ideally, information about income should relate to respondents. Instead, however, it refers to the total income of the individual's household, which in certain (exogamous) cases includes a member or members of another faith. Still, as will be discussed in the next chapter, most marriages are intrafaith, and, for those that are not, it is assumed that the respondent's income strongly affects total household income. Likewise, household income is affected by the number of members of the household and, particularly, the head of household's marital status whether married or not. These factors of marriage composition in particular, and marital status in general, are taken into account in the analysis of income determinants in the next section of this chapter.

3. Calculated from Mueller and Lane 1972.

4. Given the nature of the dependent variables that are composed of several (four) possible values that are inconsistently spaced, an ordinal logistic regression was applied.

5. The patterns of a religious group, or of defined religious groups, should be judged and evaluated against a reference group. In the U.S., at least until the middle of the twentieth century, most churches considered themselves affiliated with mainline Protestantism. Members of these denominations held leadership positions and influenced American political, economic, and cultural life. Mainline Protestantism was the driving force in American life, identified heavily with the "WASP" social core group and representative of patterns that minority groups were expected to adopt (Marty 1970; Putnam and Campbell 2010). Accordingly, here and in the multivariate analyses in the next chapters, the reference group of religious affiliation is mainline Protestants, comprising Baptists, Methodists, non-denominationalists, Lutherans, Presbyterians, Anglicans, Episcopalians, restorationists, Congregationalists, Reforms, Anabaptists, Friends, and other Protestant/nonspecific—all following the mainline tradition.

6. Insofar as differentials were found in several categories of variables, they were limited to 1 or 2 percent and should be attributed to different sampling and/or real changes during the six years that lapsed between the surveys.

3. INTERFAITH MARRIAGE

1. The data on spouse's religion are not as detailed as those of respondent's faith. In particular, one cannot distinguish among Protestants' spouses by a specific denomination of evangelical, mainline, or black; accordingly, they are presented here in one category.
2. Obviously, the more peripheral Jews ("partial Jews") one includes in the Jewish population, the higher the rate of intermarriage one will find. Still, even among the more committed Jews—those who identify as Jews by religion—intermarriage increased from 19 percent in 1990 (DellaPergola 1992) to 36 percent in 2013 (Pew Research Center 2013).
3. This is a slightly smaller loss than the one found in the 2007 Pew survey (see the section in chapter 1 titled "Religious Switching"). The differences probably trace to different ways of sampling the Jewish population and slightly different definitions of Jewish background (Jewish upbringing by religion/not religion) and current Jewish affiliation (by religion, not by religion, partial Jew).

4. RELIGIOUS IDENTIFICATION

1. For an excellent review and discussion on definitions of ethnic and group identity, see, inter alia, Henry, Arrow, and Carini 1999 and Phinney 1990.
2. The results of the 2007 RLS and the 2013 Pew Research Center Survey of U.S. Jews allow several comparisons to be made. Four main identificational variables were investigated in both surveys. The rates in frequency of attending religious services were 29 percent in 2007 and 23 percent in 2013; in the importance of religion—27 percent and 26 percent; in membership in a house of worship—39 percent and 50 percent; and in belief in God—42 percent and 34 percent, respectively. The finding in regard to the importance of religion was almost identical in the two surveys, with

differentials of 6–8 percent for religious services and belief and slightly more than 10 percent for membership. Since the question in the earlier survey was aimed at religious services in general and not necessarily participation in Jewish religious services, the somewhat higher rate of participation in 2007 than in 2013 may reflect attendance in non-Jewish services. Similarly, the differentials for membership in a house of worship (which referred to the respondent or another family member) may be attributed to the fact that, unlike in 2013, when the question related to a synagogue, in 2007 respondents in interfaith marriages most likely also considered membership in their non-Jewish spouse's church. The residual of the differences may be attributed to sampling variation and/or trends in Jewish identification in the six years between the studies.

3. Notably, the variables of each factor, i.e., measure of identification, were standardized in order to ensure uniformity in the range of their scales. For the loadings of the individual variables in each factor and the liability of internal consistency of the respective variables, see appendix A2.

4. Standardized (beta) coefficients.

5. As suggested at the beginning of this chapter, analyzing a specific population from a comparative point of view limits our focus to religious and ethnic patterns that are relevant to all groups under investigation. Obviously, however, there are other behaviors and attitudes that are particular to a single religious group and may even play an important role in their members' overall identification. In the case of Jews, such a component of identification is their attachment to Israel. Given that it relates only to Jews, Israel received no attention in the 2007 Pew survey. It should be noted that Israel is a major component in the identification of many American Jews. It was long a major form of communal consensus and, through communal institutions and pro-Israel activities, served as a social and cultural foundation and a major source of consolidation (Goldscheider 1988). Activity for Israel centered predominantly on Jewish public life, foremost in the areas of philanthropy and politics, and had relatively little effect on the private lives of most American Jews (Liebman 1991; Waxman 1992). Identification with Israel was mainly emotional and required no active involvement. To a large extent, the relations between the two communities relied on the view of Israel as the political and spiri-

tual center of the Jewish people and of American Jewry (and Diaspora Jewry more generally) as the periphery.

Over time, these relations have become more equal. This "paradigm shift" emerged from the self-perception of American Jewry as sufficiently mature, secure, and as important as Israel. Likewise, most American Jews, particularly those in positions of authority in the American Jewish communal structure, as well as those who are opinion leaders in American society at large, were born after the Holocaust and the establishment of Israel and take Israel's existence as a given (Rebhun, Waxman, and Beider 2014). From the Israeli point of view, too, Israel and the Diaspora "can no longer speak of [themselves as] a big brother and a little brother, but as two brothers walking hand in hand, supporting each other where each needs it most" (Olmert 2008). This shift has further evolved into the positions of groups and organizations that have risen in prominence and influenced the political discourse. The "official" pro-Israel lobby of American Jewry, the American Israel Public Affairs Committee (AIPAC), no longer has a monopoly on American Jewish lobbying. Other organizations, such as the "pro-Israel, pro-peace" J Street, have emerged in the United States, and the divergence emphasizes the split between American Jews on issues central to Israeli society, especially the Israeli-Palestinian conflict.

At the individual level, the empirical findings are somewhat complicated and do not necessarily point to a clear direction of change. According the 2013 Pew survey of American Jews, almost three-fourth (74 percent) defined themselves as strongly or somewhat attached to Israel, only slightly below the rate reported in 1990 (76 percent). Within the whole, however, there are significant differences among age groups: while 79 percent of Jews aged sixty-five and over are strongly or somewhat attached to Israel, this is true of only 60 percent among their young peers aged eighteen to twenty-nine. Likewise, in 2013, 46 percent of American Jews said that caring for Israel is an essential part of being Jewish, and another 44 percent termed it important but not essential (87 percent altogether). The distribution by age suggests that while 53 percent of the elderly see caring for Israel as essential to their Jewishness, only 32 percent of those below the age of thirty feel this way. It is hard to tell whether these variations by age reflect period change or cohort change, namely whether the connection to Israel is weakening over time or whether the relationship corresponds to stages in the life cycle and should be expected to strengthen as young adults marry, have children, and age. In the former case, the overall attachment to Israel will diminish; in the latter case it will remain stable and may even increase.

Meanwhile, we can add that the proportion of American Jews who have visited Israel at least once is on the rise: from 25 percent in 1990 to 47 percent in 2013, with no substantial differences among age groups. This should partly be attributed to informal educational programs that involve a visit to Israel, especially Taglit-Birthright, which targets Jews aged eighteen to twenty-six and is subsidized by the Israeli government, Jewish organizations, and philanthropists. Since such a visit often strengthens ties, the large number of young Jews who participate in one may bolster the role of Israel in their Jewish identification in both the short and the long run.

The intensity of the relationship with Israel is also affected by changes in the structure of the Jewish population. In this regard, one should mention the anticipated growth in the share of Orthodox Jews: while today they account for some 10 percent of American Jewish adults, among those below the age of eighteen the proportion of Orthodox is 27 percent. Assuming a high retention rate within Orthodoxy, the share of Orthodox among adults is expected to increase over time, boosting the overall level of attachment of American Jews toward Israel.

Finally, another important structural change is the growing number of Israelis in the United States, today accounting for some 5 percent of the total American Jewish population. Although they emigrated from Israel, they remain intimately attached to their origin country due to the presence of family and friends there, frequent visits, and, for most, speaking Hebrew at home. More recently, Israelis in the United States have begun to establish organizations and institutionalize their activities, which center on care for and activities on behalf of Israel. As Israelis continue to immigrate to the United States and increasingly consolidate around the new organizations, which may also collaborate with local Jewish organizations, American Jews' ties to Israel may gather strength as well.

5. POLITICAL ORIENTATION

1. One of the more extreme and explicit expressions of this view is the assertion made by Theodore Roosevelt in a speech he gave on May 31, 1916 (*New York Times* 1916).

REFERENCES

Abbott, Andrew. 2001. *Time Matters: On Theory and Methods*. Chicago: University of Chicago Press.

Ahlstrom, Sydney E. 1975. *A Religious History of the American People*. Garden City, NY: Doubleday.

Alba, Richard. 1990. *Ethnic Identity: The Transformation of White America*. New Haven: Yale University Press.

———. 2006. "On the Sociological Significance of the American Jewish Experience: Boundary Blurring, Assimilation, and Pluralism." *Sociology of Religion: A Quarterly Review* 67(4): 347–58.

———, and Reid M. Golden. 1986. "Patterns of Ethnic Marriage in the United States." *Social Forces* 65(1): 202–23.

———, and Victor Nee. 2003. *Remaking the American Mainstream: Assimilation and Contemporary Immigration*. Cambridge: Harvard University Press.

Albrecht, Don E. 1998. "The Industrial Transformation of Farm Communities: Implications for Family Structure and Socioeconomic Conditions." *Rural Sociology* 63(1):51–64.

Amar, Reuven, and Shlomo Toledano. 2001. *Hudap Manual with Mathematics and Windows Interface*. Jerusalem: Hebrew University of Jerusalem.

Ament, Jonathan. 2005. *American Jewish Religious Denominations*. Report Series on the National Jewish Population Survey 2000–01, no. 10. New York: United Jewish Communities.

Andersen, Robert, and Anthony Heath. 2000. *Social Cleavages, Attitudes and Voting Patterns: A Comparison of Canada and Great Britain*. Working

Paper no. 81. University of Oxford: Center for Research Into Elections and Social Trends.

Anti-Defamation League. 2013. "A Survey About Attitudes Toward Jews in America." Marttila Strategies. http://bjpa.org/publications/details.cfm ?publicationID=18493.

Antunes, Rui. 2010. "Theoretical Models of Voting Behavior." *Exedra*, no. 4.

Arzheimer, Kay, and Jurgen W. Falter. 2008. "Voter Behaviour." In *Encyclopedia of Political Behaviour*, ed. Lynda Lee Kaid and Christina Holtz-Bacha. London: Sage.

Avineri, Shlomo. 1987. "Soured Promise—a Letter to an American Friend." *Jerusalem Post*, March 10.

Aviv, Caryn, and David Shneer. 2007. "Traveling Jews, Creating Memory: Eastern Europe, Israel, and the Diaspora Business." In *Sociology Confronts the Holocaust: Memories and Identities in Jewish Diasporas*, ed. Judit M. Gerson and Diane L. Wolf, 67–83. Durham: Duke University Press.

Babchuk, Nicholas, and Hugh P. Whitt. 1990. "R-Order and Religious Switching." *Journal for the Scientific Study of Religion* 29(2): 246–54.

Bar-Lev, Mordechai, and Kedem Peri. 1986. "Uniformity and Distinctiveness in Jewish and Zionist Identity and Identification Among Israeli Students." In *Aspects of Education*, ed. Yehuda Eisenberg, 155–77. Ramat Gan: Bar-Ilan University.

Barnes, Samuel H., and Max Kaase, eds. 1979. *Political Action: Mass Participation in Five Western Democracies*. Beverly Hills: Sage.

Bartels, Larry M. 2010. "The Study of Electoral Behavior." In *The Oxford Handbook of American Elections and Political Behavior*, ed. Jan E. Leighley, 239–61. Oxford: Oxford University Press.

Beit-Hallahmi, Benjamin. 1989. *Prolegomena of the Psychological Study of Religion*. Lewisburg, PA: Bucknell University Press.

Bellah, Robert N., Richard Madsen, William M. Sullivan, Ann Swidler, and Steven M. Tipton. 1996 [1985]. *Habits of the Heart: Individualism and Commitment in American Life*. Berkeley: University of California Press.

Berger, Peter L. 1967. *The Sacred Canopy: Elements of a Sociological Theory of Religion*. Garden City, NY: Doubleday.

Borg, Ingwer, and James Lingoes. 1987. *Multidimensional Similarity Structure Analysis*. New York: Springer.

Bouvier, Leon F., and Carlo J. De Vita. 1991. "The Baby Boom—Entering Midlife." *Population Bulletin* 46, no. 3.

Brodkin, Karen. 1998. *How Jews Became White Folks and What That Says About Race in America.* New Brunswick, NJ: Rutgers University Press.

Brooks, Clem, Paul Nieuwbeerta, and Jeff Manza. 2006. "Cleavage-Based Voting Behavior in Cross-National Perspective: Evidence from Six Postwar Democracies." *Social Science Research* 35(1):88–128.

Brown, Callum G. 1992. "A Revisionist Approach to Religious Change." In *Religion and Modernisation: Sociologists and Historians Debate the Secularization Thesis,* ed. Steve Bruce, 31–89. Oxford: Clarendon.

Brown, David L., Glenn V. Fuguitt, Tim B. Heaton, and Waseem Saba. 1997. "Continuities in Size of Place Preferences in the United States, 1972–1992." *Rural Sociology* 62(4): 408–28.

Brown, David L., and W. A. Kandel. 2006. "Rural America Through a Demographic Lens." In *Population Change and Rural Society,* ed. W. A. Kandel and David L. Brown, 3–13. Dordrecht, Netherlands: Springer.

Brubaker, Rogers, and Frederick Cooper. 2000. "Beyond Identity." *Theory and Society* 29(1):1–47.

Bunin Benor, Sarah, and Steven M. Cohen. 2011. "Talking Jewish: The 'Ethnic English' of American Jews." In *Studies in Contemporary Jewry,* vol. 25: *Ethnicity and Beyond: Theories and Dilemmas of Jewish Group Demarcation,* ed. Eli Lederhendler, 62–78. New York: Oxford University Press.

Burden, Barry C., and Casey A. Klofstad. 2005. "Affect and Cognition in Party Identification." *Political Psychology* 26(6): 869–86.

Burstein, Paul. 2007. "Jewish Educational and Economic Success in the United States: A Search for Explanations." *Sociological Perspectives* 50(2): 209–28.

Buss, Arnold H., and Stephen E. Finn. 1987. "Classification of Personality Traits." *Journal of Personality and Social Psychology* 52(2):432–44.

Cadge, Wendy, and Elaine H. Ecklund. 2007. "Immigration and Religion." *Annual Review of Sociology* 33:359–79.

Campbell, Angus, and Robert L. Kahn. 1952. *The People Elect a President.* Ann Arbor: Survey Research Center, Institute for Social Research, University of Michigan.

Campbell, David E., and Robert D. Putnam. 2010. *American Grace: How Religion Divides and Unites Us.* New York: Simon and Schuster.

Carroll, Bret E. 2013. "Worlds in Space: American Religious Pluralism in Geographic Perspective." In *GODS in America: Religious Pluralism in the United States*, ed. Charles L. Cohen and Ronald L. Numbers, 56–102. New York: Oxford University Press.

Carroll, Jackson W., and Wade Clark Roof. 1993. "Introduction." In *Beyond Establishment: Protestant Identity in a Post-Protestant Age*, ed. Jackson W. Carroll and Wade Clark Roof, 11–27. Louisville, KY: Westminster/John Knox.

Casanova, Jose. 1992. "Private and Public Religion." *Social Research* 59(1): 17–58.

——. 2001. "Religion, the New Millennium, and Globalization." *Sociology of Religion: A Quarterly Review* 62(4): 415–41.

Castle, Emery N. 1998. "A Conceptual Framework for the Study of Rural Places." *American Journal of Agriculture Economy* 80(3):621–31.

Chanes, Jerome A. 1999. "Antisemitism and Jewish Security in Contemporary America: Why Can't Jews Take Yes for an Answer?" In *Jews in America: A Contemporary Reader*, ed. Roberta R. Farber and Chaim I. Waxman, 124–50. Hanover, NH: Brandeis University Press.

Chaves, Mark. 2011. *American Religion: Contemporary Trends*. Princeton: Princeton University Press.

——, and Philip S. Gorski. 2001. "Religious Pluralism and Religious Participation." *Annual Review of Sociology* 27:261–81.

Chiswick, Barry A. 1999. "The Occupational Attainment and Earnings of American Jewry, 1890–1990." *Contemporary Jewry* 20:68–98.

——. 2007. "The Occupational Attainment of American Jewry, 1990 to 2000." *Contemporary Jewry* 27:80–111.

Chiswick, Carmel U. 2014. *Judaism in Transition: How Economic Choices Shape Religious Tradition*. Stanford: Stanford University Press.

Christiano, Kevin J., William H. Swatos Jr., and Peter Kivisto. 2008. *Sociology of Religion: Contemporary Developments*. Lanham: Rowman and Littlefield.

Chua, Amy, and Jed Rubenfeld. 2014. *The Triple Package: How Three Unlikely Traits Explain the Rise and Fall of Cultural Groups in America*. New York: Penguin.

Cohen, Asher. 2006. *Non-Jewish Jews in Israel* [in Hebrew]. Jerusalem: Shalom Hartman Institute; Faculty of Law, Bar-Ilan University; Keter.

Cohen, Charles L., and Ronald L. Numbers. 2013. "Introduction." In *GODS in America: Religious Pluralism in the United States*, ed. Charles L. Cohen and Ronald L. Numbers, 1–18. New York: Oxford University Press.

Cohen, Erik H., and Reuven Amar. 2002. "External Variables as Points in Smallest Space Analysis: A Theoretical, Mathematical and Computer Based Contribution." *Bulletin deMethodologie Sociologique* 75(1):40–56.

Cohen, Shaye J. D. 1999. *The Beginnings of Jewishness: Boundaries, Varieties, Uncertainties.* Berkeley: University of California Press.

Cohen, Steven M. 1983. *American Modernity and Jewish Identity.* New York: Tavistock.

——. 1988. *American Assimilation or Jewish Revival?* Bloomington: Indiana University Press.

——. 1995. "Jewish Continuity Over Judaic Content: The Moderately Affiliated American Jew." In *The Americanization of the Jews*, ed. Robert M. Seltzer and Norman J. Cohen, 395–416. New York: New York University Press.

——. 1998. *Religious Stability and Ethnic Decline: Emerging Patterns of Jewish Identity in the United States.* New York: Florence G. Heller Jewish Community Centers Association.

——. 2003. "Jewish Identity Research in the United States: Ruminations on Concepts and Findings." In *Continuity, Commitment and Survival: Jewish Communities in the Diaspora*, ed. Sol Encel and Leslie Stein, 1–22. Westport, CT: Praeger.

——. 2005. "Engaging the Next Generation of American Jews." *Journal of Jewish Communal Service* 81(1-2):43–52.

——. 2006. *A Tale of Two Jewries: The 'Inconvenient Truth' for American Jews.* Steinhardt Foundation for Jewish Life, November 2006, http://www.bjpa.org/Publications/details.cfm?PublicationID=2908.

——. 2012. "'The Demise of the 'Good Jew': Marshall Sklare Award Lecture." *Contemporary Jewry* 32(1): 85–93.

——, and Arnold M. Eisen. 2000. *The Jew Within: Self, Family, and Community in America.* Bloomington: Indiana University Press.

Cohen, Warner. 1958. "The Politics of American Jews." In *The Jews: Social Patterns of an American Group*, ed. Marshall Sklare, 614–26. New York: Free Press.

Cohen, Yoel. 2012. "Jewish Cyber-Theology." *Communication Research Trends* 31(1): 4–13.

Connolly, Paul. 2000. "What Now for the Contact Hypothesis? Towards a New Research Agenda." *Race, Ethnicity and Education* 3(2):169–93.

Converse, Philip E. 1964. "The Nature of Belief Systems in Mass Publics." In *Ideology and Discontent*, ed. David Apter, 206–61. New York: Free Press.

Coreno, Thaddeus. 2002. "Fundamentalism as a Class Culture." *Sociology of Religion: A Quarterly Review* 63(3): 335–60.

Crockett, Alasdair, and David Voas. 2006. "Generations of Decline: Religious Change in Twentieth Century Britain." *Journal for the Social Scientific Study of Religion* 54(4): 567–84.

Dashefsky, Arnold, and Howard M. Shapiro. 1976. "Ethnic and Identity." In *Ethnic Identity in Society*, ed. Arnold Dashefsky, 5–11. Chicago: Rand McNally.

Dashefsky, Arnold, and Zachary I. Heller. 2008. *Intermarriage and Jewish Journeys in the United States.* Newton Center, MA: Hebrew College, National Center for Jewish Policy Studies.

Davidson, James D., and Ralph E. Pyle. 2011. *Rethinking Faiths: Religious Stratification in America.* Lanham: Rowman and Littlefield.

Davis, Kingsley. 1965. "The Urbanization of the Human Population." *Scientific American* 213 (3): 40–53.

Deaux, Kay. 2001. "Social Identity." In *Encyclopedia of Women and Gender*, ed. Judith Worell, 2:1059–67. San Diego, CA: Academic.

DellaPergola, Sergio. 1980. "Patterns of American Jewish Fertility." *Demography* 17(3): 261–73.

——. 1991. "New Data on Demography and Identification Among Jews in the U.S.: Trends, Inconsistencies, and Disagreements." *Contemporary Jewry* 12:67–97.

——. 2001. "Jewish Identity/Assimilation/Continuity: Approaches to a Changing Reality." *Cadernos de Lengua e Litertura Hebraica,* 17–51. Sao Paulo.

——. 2005. "Was It the Demography? A Reassessment of U.S. Jewish Population Estimates, 1945–2001." *Contemporary Jewry* 25:85–131.

——. 2008. "World Jewish Population, 2007." *American Jewish Year Book* 107:551–600.

———. 2009. "Jewish Out-Marriage: A Global Perspective." In *Jewish Intermarriage Around the World*, ed. Shulamit Reinharz and Sergio Della Pergola, 13–39. New Brunswick, NJ: Transaction.

———. 2013a. "How Many Jews in the United States? The Demographic Perspective." *Contemporary Jewry* 33(1–2): 15–42.

———. 2013b. "Bigger Population Estimate Means Wider Definition of Jewishness." *Forward*, October 11.

———. 2014a. "Jewish Demography: Some Predicaments." *Studies in Contemporary Jewry*, vol. 27: *The Social Scientific Study of Jewry: Sources, Approaches, Debates*, ed. Uzi Rebhun, 3–36. New York: Oxford University Press.

———. 2014b. "End of Jewish/Non-Jewish Dichotomy? Evidence from the 2013 Pew Survey." *American Jewish Year Book* 114:33–39.

———, and Uziel O. Schmelz. 1989. "Demographic Transformations of U.S. Jewry: Marriage and Mixed Marriage in the 1980s." *Studies in Contemporary Jewry*, vol. 5: *Israel: State and Society, 1948–1988*, ed. Peter Y. Medding, 169–200. New York: Oxford University Press.

Demerath, Nicholas J. 1965. *Social Class in American Protestantism*. Chicago: Rand Macnally.

Dershowitz, Alan M. 1997. *The Vanishing American Jew: In Search of Jewish Identity for the Next Century*. Boston: Little, Brown.

Dollinger, Marc. 2000. *Quest for Inclusion: Jews and Liberalism in Modern America*. Princeton: Princeton University Press.

Douglas, Mary. 1984. *Purity and Danger: An Analysis of the Concepts of Pollution and Taboo*. London: Ark.

Downs, Anthony. 1957. *An Economic Theory of Democracy*. New York: Harper and Row.

Durkheim, Emil. 1995 [1912]. *The Elementary Forms of the Religious Life*. New York: Free Press.

Dutwin, David, Eran Ben Porath, and Ron Miller. 2014. "U.S. Jewish Population Studies: Opportunities and Challenges." *Studies in Contemporary Jewry*, vol. 27: *The Social Scientific Study of Jewry: Sources, Approaches, Debates*, ed. Uzi Rebhun, 55–73. New York: Oxford University Press.

Dynes, Russell R. 1955. "Church-Sect Typology and Socioeconomic Status." *American Sociological Review* 20(4): 555–60.

Ebaugh, Helen R. 2003. "Religion and the New Immigrants." In *Handbook of the Sociology of Religion*, ed. Michele Dillon, 225–39. Cambridge: Cambridge University Press.

——, and Janet S. Chafetz, eds. 2002. *Religion Across Borders: Transnational Religion Networks*. Walnut Creek, CA: AltaMira.

Eck, Diana L. 2001. *A New Religious America: How a "Christian Country" Has Now Become the World's Most Religiously Diverse Nation*. San Francisco: Harper San Francisco.

Edgell, Penny. 2012. "A Cultural Sociology of Religion: New Directions." *Annual Review of Sociology* 38:247–65.

Edlin, Aaron, Andrew Gelman, and Noah Kaplan. 2007. "Voting as a Rational Choice: Why and How People Vote to Improve the Well-Being of Others." *Rationality and Society* 19(3): 293–314.

Eisen, Arnold. 2007. "Jews, Judaism, and the Problem of Hyphenated Identity in America." In *Ambivalent Jew: Charles Liebman in Memoriam*, ed. Stuart Cohen and Bernard Susser, 89–106. New York: Jewish Theological Seminary of America.

Elazar, Daniel J. 1982. "Jews on the Move: The New Wave of Jewish Migration and its Implications for Organized Jewry." *Journal of Jewish Communal Service* 58(4): 279–83.

Emerson, Michael O., and Laura J. Essenburg. 2013. *Religious Change and Continuity in the United States, 2006–2012*. Houston: Kinder Institute for Urban Research, Rice University.

Erikson, Erik H. 1963. *Childhood and Society*. 2d ed. New York: Norton.

——. 1965. "The Concept of Identity in Race Relations: Notes and Queries." In *The Negro American*, ed. T. Parsons and K. B. Clark, 227–53. Boston: Beacon.

——. 1968. *Identity: Youth and Crisis*. New York: Norton.

Erikson, Robert, and John H. Goldthorpe. 1992. *The Constant Flux: A Study of Class Mobility in Industrial Societies*. Oxford: Clarendon.

Etzioni, Amitai. 2004. "Holidays and Rituals: Neglected Seedbeds of Virtue." In *We Are What We Celebrate: Understanding Holidays and Rituals*, ed. Amitai Etzioni and Jared Bloom, 1–40. New York: New York University Press.

Evans, John H. 2013. "Religious Pluralism in Modern America: A Sociological Overview." In *GODS in America: Religious Pluralism in the United*

States, ed. Charles L. Cohen and Ronald L. Numbers, 43–55. New York: Oxford University Press.

Fearon, James D. 1999. *What Is Identity (As We Now Use the Word)*. Mimeo, https://web.stanford.edu/group/fearon-research/cgi-bin/wordpress/wp-content/uploads/2013/10/What-is-Identity-as-we-now-use-the-word-.pdf.

Feingold, Henry L. 2014. *American Jewish Political Culture and the Liberal Persuasion*. Syracuse: Syracuse University Press.

Finke, Roger. 1989. "Demographics of Religious Participation: An Ecological Approach, 1850–1980." *Journal for the Scientific Study of Religion* 28(1): 45–58.

——, and Rodney Stark. 1992. *The Churching of America, 1776–1990: Winner and Loser in Our Religious Economy*. New Brunswick, NJ: Rutgers University Press.

Fischer, Alan M. 1981. "Jewish Political Shift? Erosion, Yes; Conversion, No." In *Party Coalitions in the 1980s*, ed. Seymour M. Lipset, 327–40. San Francisco: Institute for Contemporary Studies.

Fischer, Claude S., and Michael Hout. 2006. *Century of Difference: How America Changed in the Last One Hundred Years*. New York: Russell Sage Foundation.

Fishbein, Martin, and Icek Ajzen. 1975. *Belief, Attitude, Intention and Behavior: An Introduction to Theory and Research*. Reading, MA: Addison-Wesley.

Fishman, Sylvia B. 2000. *Jewish Life and American Culture*. Albany: State University of New York Press.

——. 2004. *Double or Nothing? Jewish Families and Mixed Marriage*. Hanover, NH: Brandeis University Press.

Forman, Ira N. 2001. "The Historical Voting Behavior of American Jews." In *Jews in American Politics*, ed. L. Sandy Maisel, Ira N. Forman, Donald Altschiller, and Charles W. Bassett, 141–60. Lanham: Rowman and Littlefield.

Freedman, Samuel G. 2000. *Jew vs. Jew: The Struggle for the Soul of American Jewry*. New York: Touchstone.

Fuchs, Lawrence. 1956. *The Political Behavior of American Jews*. Glencoe, IL: Free Press.

Galkina, Helen. 1996. "Theoretical Approaches to Ethnic Identity." http://lucy.ukc.ac.uk/csacpub/russian/galkina.html.

Gan, Katheine N., Patty Jacobson, Gil Preuss, and Barry Shrage. 2008. *The 2005 Greater Boston Community Study: Intermarried Families and Their Children.* Boston: Combined Jewish Philanthropies.

Gans, Herbert J. 1994. "Symbolic Ethnicity and Symbolic Religiosity: Towards a Comparison of Ethnic and Religious Acculturation." *Ethnic and Racial Studies* 17(4): 577–92.

Geertz, Clifford. 1963. "The Integrative Revolution: Primordial Sentiments and Politics in the New States." In *Old Societies and New States: The Quest for Modernity in Asia and Africa,* ed. Clifford Geertz, 105–57. New York: Free Press.

——. 1973. *The Interpretation of Cultures: Selected Essays.* New York: Basic Books.

Geffen Mintz, Rela. 2005. "Life-Cycle Rituals: Rites of Passage in American Judaism." In *The Cambridge Companion to American Judaism,* ed. Dana Evan Kaplan, 225–35. New York: Cambridge University Press.

Ginsberg, Benjamin. 2001. "Dilemmas of Jewish Leadership in America." In *Jews in American Politics* ed. Sandy Maisel, and Ira N. Forman, 3–27. Lanham: Rowman and Littlefield.

Goldscheider, Calvin. 1967. "Fertility of the Jews." *Demography* 4(1): 196–209.

——. 1986. *Jewish Continuity and Change: Emerging Patterns in America.* Bloomington: Indiana University Press.

——. 1988. "Who Is a Jew? Why Are American Jews in Uproar?" [in Hebrew] *Gesher: Journal of Jewish Affairs* 119:37–45.

——. 2004. *Studying the Jewish Future.* Seattle: University of Washington Press.

——. 2010. "Boundary Maintenance and Jewish Identity: Comparative and Historical Perspectives." In: *Boundaries of Jewish Identity,* ed. Susan A. Glenn and Noami B. Sokoloff, 110–31. Seattle: University of Washington Press.

——, and Alan S. Zuckerman. 1984. *The Transformation of the Jews.* Chicago: University of Chicago Press.

Goldstein, Eric L. 2006. *The Price of Whiteness: Jews, Race, and American Identity.* Princeton: Princeton University Press.

Goldstein, Sidney. 1969. "Socioeconomic Differentials among Religious Groups in the United States." *American Journal of Sociology* 74(5): 612–31.

——. 1981. "Jews in the United States: Perspectives from Demography." *American Jewish Year Book* 81:3–59.

——. 1982. "Population Movement and Redistribution Among American Jews." *Jewish Journal of Sociology* 24 (June): 5–23.

——. 1991. "American Jews on the Move." *Moment* 16(4): 24–29, 49–51.

——. 1992. "Profile of American Jewry: Insights from the 1990 National Jewish Population Survey. *American Jewish Year Book*, 92:77–173.

——, and Alice Goldstein. 1996. *Jews on the Move: Implications for Jewish Identity*. Albany: State University of New York Press.

Gordon, Milton M. 1964. *Assimilation in American Life: The Role of Race, Religion, and National Origins*. New York: Oxford University Press.

Greeley, Andrew M. 1972. *The Denominational Society: A Sociological Approach to Religion in America*. Glenview, IL: Scott, Foresman.

——. 1977. *The American Catholic: A Social Portrait*. New York: Basic Books.

——. 1989. *Religious Change in America*. Cambridge: Harvard University Press.

——. 1998. "Foreword." In *Jewish Choices: American Jewish Denominationalism*, ed. Bernard Lazerwitz, J. Alan Winter, Arnold Dashefsky, and Ephraim Tabory. Albany: State University of New York Press.

Green, Donald P., and Bradley L. Palmquist. 1990. "Of Artifacts and Partisan Instability." *American Journal of Political Science* 34(3): 872–902.

Greene, Steven. 2004. "Social Identity Theory and Party Identification." *Social Science Quarterly* 85(1):136–53.

Guttman, Louis. 1959a. "Introduction to Facet Design and Analysis." In *Proceedings of the Fifteenth International Congress of Psychology, Brussels 1957*, 130–32. Amsterdam.

——. 1959b. "A Structural Theory for Intergroup Beliefs and Action." *American Sociological Review* 24(3): 318–28.

——. 1968. "A General Nonmetric Technique for Finding the Smallest Coordinate Space for a Configuration of Points." *Psychometrika* 33(4): 469–506.

Habermas, Jurgen. 2006. "Religion in the Public Sphere." *European Journal of Philosophy* 14(1): 1–25.

Hagan, Jacqueline, and Helen R. Ebaugh. 2003. "Calling Upon the Sacred: Migrants' Use of Religion in the Migration Process." *International Migration Review* 37(4):1145–62.

Hansen, Marcus L. 1938. *The Problem of the Third Generation Immigrant*. Rock Island, IL: Augustana Historical Society.

Hartman, Harriet, and Moshe Hartman. 2009. *Gender and American Jews: Patterns in Work, Education, and Family in Contemporary Life.* Waltham, MA: Brandeis University Press.

Hartman, Harriet, and Ira Sheskin. 2012. "The Relationship of Jewish Community Contexts and Jewish Identity: A 22-Community Study." *Contemporary Jewry* 32 (3): 237–83.

Hartman, Moshe, and Harriet Hartman. 1996. *Gender Equality and American Jews.* Albany: State University of New York Press.

Heer, David M. 1980. "Intermarriage." In *Harvard Encyclopedia of American Ethnic Groups*, ed. Stephan Thernstrom, Ann Orlov, and Oscar Handlin, 513–21. Cambridge: Belknap.

Heilman, Samuel C. 1995. *Portrait of American Jews: The Last Half of the Twentieth Century.* Seattle: University of Washington Press.

Henry, Kelly B., Holly Arrow, and Barbara Carini. 1999. "A Tripartite Model of Group Identification: Theory and Measurement." *Small Group Research* 30(5): 558–81.

Herberg, Will. 1983 [1955]. *Protestant-Catholic-Jew: An Essay in American Religious Sociology.* Chicago: University of Chicago Press.

Herman, Simon N. 1977. *Jewish Identity: A Social Psychological Perspective.* Beverly Hills: Sage.

Himmelfarb, Harold, and R. Michael Loar. 1984. "National Trends in Jewish Ethnicity: A Test of the Polarization Hypothesis." *Journal of the Scientific Study of Religion* 23(2): 140–54.

Hirschman, Charles. 2004. "The Role of Religion in the Origins and Adaptation of Immigrant Groups in the United States." *International Migration Review* 38(3): 1206–33.

Hoge, Dean R. 1979. "A Test of Theories of Denominational Growth and Decline." In *Understanding Church Growth and Decline, 1950–1978*, ed. Dean R. Hoge and David A. Roozen, 179–97. New York: Pilgrim.

Hogg, Michael A., and Dominic Abrams. 1988. *Social Identification: A Social Psychology of Intergroup Relations and Group Processes.* New York: Routledge.

Hollinger, David A. 1997. "Jewish Intellectuals and the De-Christianization of American Public Culture in the Twentieth Century." In *New Directions in American Religious History*, ed. Harry S. Stout and Darryl G. Hart, 462–84. New York: Oxford University Press.

Horowitz, Bethamie. 2003. *Connections and Journeys: Assessing Critical Opportunities for Enhancing Jewish Identity.* New York: UJA–Federation of New York.

———. 2011. "Old Casks in New Times: The Reshaping of American Jewish Identity in the Twenty-first Century." In *Studies in Contemporary Jewry,* vol. 25: *Ethnicity and Beyond: Theories and Dilemmas of Jewish Group Demarcation,* ed. Eli Lederhendler, 79–90. New York: Oxford University Press.

Hout, Michael. 2003. "Demographic Methods for the Sociology of Religion." In *Handbook of the Sociology of Religion,* ed. Michele Dillon, 79–84. Cambridge: Cambridge University Press.

———, and Claude S. Fischer. 2002. "Why More Americans Have No Religious Preference: Politics and Generations." *American Sociological Review* 67(2): 165–90.

———, Andrew, Greeley, and Melissa J. Wilde. 2001. *The Demographic Imperative in Religious Change in the United States.* GSS Social Change Report, no. 45.

Howe, Irving. 1976. *World of Our Fathers: The Journey of the East European Jews to America and the Life They Found and Made.* New York: Harcourt, Brace, Jovanovich.

Huckfeldt, Robert, and John Sprague. 1995. *Citizens, Politics, and Social Communication: Information and Influence in an Election Campaign.* New York: Cambridge University Press.

Hudson, Winthrop S. 1965. *Religion in America.* New York: Scribner's.

Hunter, James D. 1983. *American Evangelicalism: Conservative Religion and the Quandary of Modernity.* New Brunswick, NJ: Rutgers University Press.

Isaacs, Harold R. 1975. "Basic Group Identity: The Idols of the Tribe." In *Ethnicity: Theory and Experience,* ed. Nathan Glazar and Daniel P. Moynihan, 29–52. Cambridge: Harvard University Press.

Jackman, Mary R., and Marie Crane. 1986. "Some of My Best Friends Are Black . . . : Interracial Friendship and Whites' Racial Attitudes." *Public Opinion Quarterly* 50(4): 459–86.

Jacobson, Matthew F. 2002. *Special Sorrows: The Diasporic Imagination of Irish, Polish, and Jewish Immigrants in the United States.* Berkeley: University of California Press.

James, William. 1890. *The Principles of Psychology*. Vol. 1. New York: Holt.

Jenkins, Philip. 2002. "A New Religious America." *First Things*, no. 125 (August/September): 25–28.

Kadushin, Charles, Benjamin T. Phillips, and Leonard Saxe. 2005. "National Jewish Population Survey 2000–01: A Guide for the Perplexed." *Contemporary Jewry* 25:1–32.

——, Graham Wright, Michelle Shain, and Leonard, Saxe. 2012. "How Socially Integrated Into Mainstream America Are Young American Jews?" *Contemporary Jewry* 32(2): 167–87.

Kalmijn, Matthijs. 1993. "Trends in Black/White Intermarriage." *Social Forces* 72(1): 119–46.

——. 1998. "Intermarriage and Homogamy: Causes, Patterns, Trends." *Annual Review of Sociology* 24:395–421.

——. 2010. "Consequences of Racial Intermarriage for Children's Social Integration." *Sociological Perspectives* 53(2): 271–86.

Kammen, Michael. 1986. *Spheres of Liberty: Changing Perceptions of Liberty in America Culture*. Madison: University of Wisconsin Press.

Kaplan, Dana Evan. 2005. "Trends in American Judaism from 1945 to the Present." In *The Cambridge Companion to American Judaism*, ed. Dana Evan Kaplan, 61–78. New York: Cambridge University Press.

——. 2009. *Contemporary American Judaism: Transformation and Renewal*. New York: Columbia University Press.

Kaufman, Debra Renee. 2007. "Post-Memory and Post-Holocaust Jewish Identity Narratives." In *Sociology Confronts the Holocaust: Memories and Identities in Jewish Diasporas*, ed. Judit M. Gerson and Diane L. Wolf, 39–54. Durham: Duke University Press.

Kelley, Dean M. 1972. *Why Conservative Churches Are Growing*. New York: Harper and Row.

Kellstedt, Lyman A. 1993. "Religion, the Neglected Variable: An Agenda for Future Research on Religion and Political Behavior." In *Rediscovering the Religious Factor in American Politics*, ed. David C. Leege and Lyman A. Kellstedt, 273–303. New York: Routledge.

Killian, Caitlin E. 2001. "Cultural Choices and Identity Negotiation of Muslim Maghrebin Women in France." Ph.D. diss., Atlanta: Emory University.

Kim, Helen, and Noah Leavitt. 2012. "The Newest Jews? Understanding Jew-ish American and Asian American Marriages." *Contemporary Jewry* 32(2): 135–66.

Knoke, Daniel. 1974. "A Causal Synthesis of Sociological and Psychological Models of American Voting Behavior." *Social Forces* 53(1): 92–101.

Knusten, Oddbjorn. 2006. *Class Voting in Western Europe: A Comparative Lon-gitudinal Study*. Lanham, MD: Lexington.

Kosmin, Barry A. 2014. "It's the Best of Times: It's the Worst of Times." *American Jewish Year Book*, 114:61–66.

——, Sidney Goldstein, Joseph Waksberg, Nava Lerer, Ariella Keysar, and Jeffrey Scheckner. 1991. *Highlights of the CJF 1990 National Jewish Popula-tion Survey*. New York: Council of Jewish Federations.

——, and Ariela Keysar. 2006. *Religion in a Free Market: Religious and Non-Religious Americans—Who, What, Why, Where*. Ithaca, NY: Paramount.

——, and Seymour P. Lachman. 1993. *One Nation Under God: Religion in Contemporary American Society*. New York: Harmony.

Kotler-Berkowiyz, Laurence, Steven M. Cohen, Jonathan Ament, Vivian Klaff, Frank Mott, and Danyelle Peckerman-Neuman. 2003. *The National Jewish Population Survey 2000–01: Strength, Challenge and Diversity in the American Jewish Population*. New York: United Jewish Communities.

Kredo, Adam. 2015. "Allies Accuse Jewish Lawmakers of Dual Loyalty to Israel." *Washington Free Beacon*, August 8.

Kristol, Irving. 1988. "Liberalism and American Jews." *Commentary* (Octo-ber): 19–23.

——. 1990. "The Liberal Tradition of American Jews." In *American Pluralism and the Jewish Community*, ed. Seymour M. Lipset, 109–16. New Bruns-wick, NJ: Transaction.

Lazarsfeld, Paul F., Bernard Berelson, and Hazel Gaudet. 1944. *The People's Choice: How the Voter Makes Up His Mind in a Presidential Campaign*. New York: Duell, Sloan and Pearce.

Lazerwitz, Bernard. 1977. "The Community Variable in Jewish Identification." *Journal for the Scientific Study of Religion* 16(4): 361–69.

——, J. Alan Winter, Arnold Dashefsky, and Ephraim Tabory. 1998. *Jewish Choices: American Jewish Denominationalism*. Albany: State University of New York Press.

Lee, Everett S. 1966. "A Theory of Migration." *Demography* 3(1): 47–57.

Lefkowitz, Jay P. 1993. "Jewish Voters and the Democrats." *Commentary* 95 (April): 38–41.

Legge, Jerome. 1995. "Explaining Jewish Liberalism in the United States: An Exploration of Socioeconomic, Religious, and Communal Living Variables." *Social Science Quarterly* 76(1): 124–41.

Lehrer, Evelyn L. 1995. "The Effect of Religion on the Labor Supply of Married Women." *Social Science Research* 24(3): 281–301.

——. 1998. "Religious Intermarriage in the United States: Determinants and Trends." *Social Science Research* 27(3): 245–63.

——. 2004. "Religious as a Determinant of Economic and Demographic Behavior in the U.S." *Population and Development Review* 30(4): 707–26.

——, and Carmel U. Chiswick. 1993. "Religion as a Determinant of Marital Stability." *Demography* 30(3): 385–404.

Lenski, Gerhard E. 1961. *The Religious Factor: A Sociological Study of Religion's Impact on Politics, Economics, and Family Life*. Garden City, NY: Doubleday.

Lerner, Robert, Althea K. Nagai, and Stanley Rothman. 1989. "Marginality and Liberalism among Jewish Elite." *Public Opinion Quarterly* 53(3): 330–52.

Levy, Geoffrey B. 1995. *Toward a Theory of Disproportionate American Jewish Liberalism*. New York: Oxford University Press.

Levy, Shlomit. 1985. "Lawful Roles of Facets in Social Theories." in *Facet Theory: Approaches to Social Research*, ed. David Canter, 59–69. New York: Springer.

——. 2009. "Trends in Jewish Identity in Israeli Society: Effects of Former Soviet Union Immigration." *Contemporary Jewry* 29(2): 153–68.

Lichter, Daniel T., and David L. Brown. 2011. "Rural America in an Urban Society: Changing Spatial and Social Boundaries." *Annual Review of Sociology* 37:565–92.

Lieberson, Stanley, and Mary C. Waters. 1988. *From Many Strands: Ethnic and Racial Groups in Contemporary America*. New York: Russell Sage Foundation.

Liebman, Arthur. 1979. *Jews and the Left*. New York: Wiley.

Liebman, Charles S. 1973. *The Ambivalent American Jew: Politics, Religion, and Family in American Jewish Life*. Philadelphia: Jewish Publication Society of America.

———. 1989. "The Quality of American Jewish Life: A Grim Outlook." In *Facing the Future: Essays on Contemporary Jewish Life*, ed. Steven S. Bayme, 50–71. New York: Ktav and the American Jewish Committee.

———. 1991. "Religious Trends Among Jews in the U.S.A. and Israel and Changing Images of Israel." *Contemporary Jewry: A Research Annual* [*Yahadut Z'emanenu*] 7:243–62 [in Hebrew].

Lipset, Seymour M. 1960. *Political Man: The Social Basis of Politics*. Garden City, NY: Doubleday.

———. 1971. "The Socialism of Fools: The Left, the Jews, and Israel." In *The New Left and the Jews*, ed. Mordechai S. Chertoff, 103–31. New York: Pitman.

———. 1972. *Group Life in America: A Task Force Report*. New York: American Jewish Committee.

———, and Earl Raab. 1995. *Jews and the New American Scene*. Cambridge: Harvard University Press.

London, Perry, and Allissa Hirschfeld. 1991. "The Psychology of Identity Formation." In *Jewish Identity in America*, ed. D. M. Gordis and Y. Ben-Horin, 31–50. Los Angeles: Wilstein Institute of Jewish Policy Studies.

Loveland, Matthew T. 2003. "Religious Switching: Preference, Development, Maintenance and Change." *Journal for the Scientific Study of Religion* 42(1): 147–58.

Machacek, David W. 2003. "The Problem of Pluralism." *Sociology of Religion: A Quarterly Review* 64(2): 145–61.

Mack, Raymond W., Raymond J. Murphy, and Seymour Yellin. 1956. "The Protestant Ethic, Level of Aspiration, and Social Mobility: An Empirical Test." *American Sociological Review* 21(3): 295–300.

Madsen, Richard. 2009. "The Archipelago of Faith: Religious Individualism and Faith Community in America Today." *American Journal of Sociology* 114(5): 1263–301.

Magid, Shaul. 2013. *American Post-Judaism: Identity and Renewal in a Postethnic Society*. Bloomington: Indiana University Press.

Manza, Jeff, and Nathan Wright. 2003. "Religion and Political Behavior." In *Handbook of the Sociology of Religion*, ed. Michele Dillon, 297–314. Cambridge: Cambridge University Press.

Marsh, Robert M. 1966. "Comparative Sociology, 1950–1963." *Current Sociology* 14(2): 5–34.

Marty, Martin E. 1970. *Righteous Empire: The Protestant Experience in America.* New York: Dial.

———. 1986. *Under God, Indivisible, 1941–1960,* vol. 3 of *Modern American Religion.* Chicago: University of Chicago Press.

Marx, Karl. 1978. "Contribution to the Critique of Hegel's Philosophy of Right." In *The Marx-Engels Reader,* ed. R. C. Tucker, 53–65. New York: Norton.

Massarik, Fred. 1977. "The Boundary of Jewishness: Some Measures of Jewish Identity in the United States." In *Papers in Jewish Demography 1973,* ed. Uziel O. Schmelz, Paul Glikson, and Sergio DellaPergola, 117–39. Jerusalem: Institute of Contemporary Jewry, Hebrew University of Jerusalem.

Mayer, Albert J., and Harry Sharp. 1962. "Religious Preference and Worldly Success." *American Sociological Review* 27(2): 218–27.

Mayer, Egon, Barry A. Kosmin, and Ariela Keysar. 2002. *American Jewish Identity Survey 2001-AJIS: Report-An Exploration in the Demographic and Outlook of a People.* New York: Center for Cultural Judaism.

McFarland, Michael J., Bradley R. E. Wright, and David L. Weakliem. 2011. "Educational Attainment and Religiosity: Exploring Variations by Religious Tradition." *Sociology of Religion: A Quarterly Review* 72(2): 166–68.

McGuire, Meredith. 2001. *Religion: The Social Context.* 5th ed. Belmont, CA: Wadsworth/Thomson Learning.

McPherson, Miller, Lynn Smith-Lovin, and James Cook. 2001. "Birds of a Feather: Homophily in Social Networks." *Annual Review of Sociology* 27:415–44.

Medding, Peter Y. 1977. "Towards a General Theory of Jewish Political Interests and Behavior." *Jewish Journal of Sociology* 19(2): 115–44.

———, Gary A. Tobin, Sylvia B. Fishman, and Mordechai Rimor. 1992. "Jewish Identity in Conversionary and Mixed Marriage." *American Jewish Year Book,* 92:3–76.

Miller, Daniel R. 1963. "The Study of Social Relationships: Situation, Identity, and Social Interaction." In *Psychology: A Study of a Science,* ed. S. Koch, 5:639–737. New York: McGraw-Hill.

Mueller, Samuel A., and Angela V. Lane. 1972. "Tabulations from the 1957 Current Population Survey on Religion: A Contribution to the Demography of American Religion." *Journal for the Scientific Study of Religion* 11(1): 76–98.

New York Times. 1916. June 1, p. 4.

Niebuhr, H. Richard. 1929. *The Social Sources of Denominationalism.* New York: Henry Holt.

O'Leary, Richard, and Fjalar Finnas. 2002. "Education, Social Integration, and Minority-Majority Group Intermarriage." *Sociology* 36(2): 235–54.

Olmert, Ehud. 2008. "Address of Prime Minister Ehud Olmert to the Board of Governors Plenum," June 22, http://www.pmo.gov.il/English/Media-Center/Speeches/Pages/speechagency220608.aspx.

Olson, M. 1965. *The Logic of Collective Action.* Cambridge: Harvard University Press.

Owens, Timothy J., Dawn T. Robinson, and Lynn Smith-Lovin. 2010. "Three Faces of Identity." *Annual Review of Sociology* 36:477–99.

Park, Jerry Z., and Samuel H. Reimer. 2002. "Revisiting the Social Sources of American Christianity, 1972–1998." *Journal for the Scientific Study of Religion* 41(4): 733–46.

Park, Robert E. 1928. "Human Migration and the Marginal Man." *American Journal of Sociology* 33(6): 881–93.

Perl, Paul, and Daniel V. A. Olson. 2000. "Religious Market Share and Intensity of Church Involvement in Five Denominations." *Journal for the Scientific Study of Religion* 39(1): 12–31.

Perlman, Joel, and Roger Waldinger. 1997. "Second Generation Decline? Children of Immigrants, Past and Present—a Reconsideration." *International Migration Review* 31(4): 893–922.

Perlmutter, Philip. 1996. *The Dynamics of American Ethnic, Religious, and Racial Group Life: An Interdisciplinary Overview.* Westport, CT: Praeger.

Pew Forum. 2008. *U.S. Religious Landscape Survey: Religious Affiliation-Diverse and Dynamics.* Washington, DC: Pew Research Center.

Pew Research Center. 2004. *Religion and the Presidential Vote.* Washington, DC: Pew Research Center.

——. 2011. *Religious and Public Life Project: The Future of the Global Muslim Population.* Washington, DC: Pew Research Center.

——. 2012. *How the Faithful Voted: 2012 Preliminary Analysis.* http://www.pewforum.org/2012/11/07/how-the-faithful-voted-2012-preliminary-exit-poll-analysis/.

——. 2013. *A Portrait of Jewish Americans: Findings from a Pew Research Center Survey of U.S. Jews.* Washington, DC: Pew Research Center.

Phillips, Benjamin T., and Sylvia Barack Fishman. 2006. "Ethnic Capital and Intermarriage: A Case Study of American Jews." *Sociology of Religion: A Quarterly Review* 67(4): 487–505.

Phillips, Bruce. 2005. "American Judaism in the Twenty-First Century." In *The Cambridge Companion to American Judaism*, ed. Dana Evan Kaplan, 397–415. New York: Cambridge University Press.

Phinney, Jean S. 1990. "Ethnic Identity in Adolescents and Adults: Review of Research." *Psychological Bulletin* 108(3): 499–514.

Prell, Riv-Ellen. 1989. *Prayer and Community: The Havurah in American Judaism*. Detroit: Wayne State University Press.

Putnam, Robert D. 2000. *Bowling Alone: The Collapse and Revival of American Community*. New York: Simon and Schuster.

——, and David E. Campbell. 2010. *American Grace: How Religion Divides and Unites Us*. New York: Simon and Schuster.

Pyle, Ralph E. 2006. "Trends in Religious Stratification: Have Religious Group Socioeconomic Distinctions Declined in Recent Decades?" *Sociology of Religion: A Quarterly Review* 67(1): 61–79.

Qian, Zhenchao, and Daniel T. Lichter. 2007. "Social Boundaries and Marital Assimilation: Interpreting Trends in Racial and Ethnic Intermarriage." *American Sociological Review* 72(1): 68–95.

Rapaport, Lynn. 2005. "The Holocaust in American Jewish Life." In *The Cambridge Companion to American Judaism*, ed. Dana Evan Kaplan, 187–208. New York: Cambridge University Press.

Rebhun, Uzi. 1993. "Trends in the Size of American Jewish Denominations: A Renewed Evaluation." *CCAR Journal: A Reform Jewish Quarterly* 40 (1): 1–11.

——. 1995. "The Distance of the Jewish Community from Its Institutions: The Case of Jewish Schools." *Journal of Jewish Communal Service* 71(2–3): 221–33.

——. 1997a. *Geographic Mobility and Religioethnic Identification Among American Jews, 1970–1990* [in Hebrew]. Ph.D. diss., Hebrew University of Jerusalem.

——. 1997b. "Changing Patterns of Internal Migration, 1970–1990: A Comparative Analysis of Jews and Whites in the United States." *Demography* 34(2): 213–23.

——. 1999. "Jewish Identification in Intermarriage: Does a Spouse's Religion (Catholic vs. Protestant) Matter?" *Sociology of Religion: A Quarterly Review* 60(1): 71–88.

——. 2002. "Directions, Magnitude, and Efficiency of Interregional Migration, 1970–1990: Jews and Whites in the United States Compared." *Review of Regional Studies* 32(1): 37–68.

——. 2004. "Jewish Identification in Contemporary America: Gans's Symbolic Ethnicity and Religiosity Theory Revisited." *Social Compass: International Review of Sociology of Religion* 51(3): 349–66.

——. 2011. "Migration, Time, and Religioethnic Identification Among U.S. Jews." *Sociological Forum* 26(2): 306–33.

——. 2014. "Correlates of Experiences and Perceptions of Anti-Semitism Among Jews in the United States." *Social Science Research* 47 (September): 44–60.

——, and Sidney Goldstein. 2006. "Changes in the Geographic Dispersion and Mobility of American Jews, 1990–2001." *Jewish Journal of Sociology* 48(1, 2): 5–33.

——, and Lilach Lev Ari. 2010. *American Israelis: Migration, Transnationalism, and Diasporic Identity*. Boston: Brill.

——, Chaim I. Waxman, and Nadia Beider. 2014. "American Jews and the Israeli-Palestinian Peace Process: A Study of Diaspora in International Affairs". In *Reconsidering Israel-Diaspora Relations*, ed. Eliezer Ben-Rafael, Judit Bokser Liwerant, and Yosef Gorny, 334–66. Leiden: Brill.

Reimer, Samuel. 2007. "Class and Congregations: Class and Religious Affiliation at the Congregational Level and Analysis." *Journal for the Scientific Study of Religion* 46(4): 583–94.

Ritchey, P. Neal. 1975. "The Effect of Minority Group Status on Fertility: A Reexamination of Concepts." *Population Studies* 29(2): 249–57.

Roberts, Keith A. 1990. *Religion in Sociological Perspective*. 2d ed. Belmont, CA: Wadsworth.

Robertson, R. 1970. *The Sociological Interpretation of Religion*. Oxford: Blackwell.

Romano, Renne C. 2003. *Race Mixing: Black-White Marriage in Postwar America*. Cambridge: Harvard University Press.

Roof, Wade C. 1993. *A Generation of Seekers: The Spiritual Journey of the Baby Boom Generation*. New York: Harper Collins.

———. 2003. "Religion and Spirituality: Toward an Integrated Analysis." In *Handbook of the Sociology of Religion*, ed. Michele Dillon, 137–48. Cambridge: Cambridge University Press.

———, and William McKinney. 1987. *American Mainline Religion: Its Changing Shape and Future*. New Brunswick, NJ: Rutgers University Press.

Rosenberg, Bernard, and Irving Howe. 1976. "Are the Jews Turning Toward the Right?" In *The New Conservatives: A Critique from the Left*, ed. Irving Howe and Lewis A. Coser, 64–89. New York: New American Library.

Ryan, W. 1981. *Equality*. New York: Pantheon.

Sanders, David. 2003. "Party Identification, Economic Perceptions, and Voting in British General Elections, 1974–1997." *Electoral Studies* 22(2): 239–63.

Sandomirsky, Sharon, and John Wilson. 1990. "Processes of Disaffiliation: Religious Mobility Among Men and Women." *Social Forces* 68(4): 1211–29.

Sarna, Jonathan D. 2004. *American Judaism: A History*. New Haven: Yale University Press.

Sasson, Theodore. 2013. "New Analysis of Pew Data: Children of Intermarriage Increasingly Identify as Jews." *Tablet Magazine*, November 11, tabletmag.com/jewish-news-and-politics/151506/young-jews-opt-in.

———. 2014. "Invest in the Children of Intermarriage." *Jewish Philanthropy*, August 13, ejewish philanthropy.com/invest-in-the-children-of-intermarriage.

———, Charles Kadushin, and Leonard Saxe. 2010. "Trends in American Attachment to Israel: An Assessment of the 'Distancing' Hypothesis." *Contemporary Jewry* 30(2): 297–319.

Saxe, Leonard. 2013. "Pew Findings Reject Bleak Narrative of Jewish Decline." *Forward*, October 11.

———, Theodore Sasson, and Janet Krasner Aronson. 2014. "Pew's Portrait of American Jewry: A Reassessment of the Assimilation Narrative." *American Jewish Year Book* 114:71–81.

———, Elisabeth Tighe, and Matthew Boxer. 2014. "Measuring the Size and Characteristics of American Jewry: A New Paradigm to Understand an Ancient People." In *Studies in Contemporary Jewry*, vol. 27: *The Social Scientific Study of Jewry: Sources, Approaches, Debates*, ed. Uzi Rebhun, 37–54. New York: Oxford University Press.

Schmelz, Uziel O., and Sergio DellaPergola. 1983. "The Demographic Consequences of U.S. Jewish Population Trends." *American Jewish Year Book*, 83:141–87.

Schneider, William. 1981. "Democrats and Republicans, Liberals and Conservatives." In *Party Coalitions in the 1980s*, ed. Seymour M. Lipset, 179–231. San Francisco: Institute for Contemporary Studies.

Schwadel, Philip. 2011. "The Effects of Education on Americans' Religious Practices, Beliefs, and Affiliation." *Review of Religious Research* 53 (2): 161–82.

——. 2013. "Changes in Americans' Strength of Religious Affiliation, 1974–2010." *Sociology of Religion: A Quarterly Review* 74(1): 107–28.

——. 2014. "Are White Evangelical Protestants Lower Class? A Partial Test of Church-Sect Theory." *Social Science Research* 46 (July): 100–16.

Seltzer, Robert M., and Norman J. Cohen, eds. 1995. *The Americanization of the Jews*. New York: New York University Press.

Shandler, Jeffrey. 2009. *Jews, God, and Videotape: Religion and Media in America*. New York: New York University Press.

Shapiro, Edward S. 1992. *A Time of Healing: American Jewry since World War II*. Baltimore: Johns Hopkins University Press.

Sharot, Stephen. 2011. *Comparative Perspectives on Judaism and Jewish Identities*. Detroit: Wayne State University Press.

Sherkat, Darren E. 2002. "African-American Religious Affiliation in the Late Twentieth Century: Cohort Variation and Patterns of Switching, 1973–1998." *Journal for the Scientific Study of Religion* 41(3): 485–93.

——, and John Wilson. 1995. "Preferences, Constraints, and Choices in Religious Markets: An Examination of Religious Switching and Apostasy." *Social Forces* 73(3): 993–1026.

Sheskin, Iram, and Arnold Dashefsky. 2008. "Jewish Population in the United States, 2008." *American Jewish Year Book* 108:151–222.

Sheskin, Iram, and Micha Liben. 2015. "The People of the Nook: Jewish Use of the Internet." In *The Changing World Religion Map: Sacred Places, Identities, Practices, and Politics*, ed. Stanley D. Brunn, 3831–56. Dordrecht: Springer.

Shye, Samuel. 1978. *Theory Construction and Data Analysis in the Behavioral Sciences*. San Francisco: Jossey-Bass.

Sigalow, Emily, Michelle Shain, and Meredith Bergey. 2012. "Religion and Decisions About Marriage, Residence, Occupation, and Children." *Journal for the Scientific Study of Religion* 51(2): 304–23.

Silberman, Charles E. 1985. *A Certain People: American Jews and Their Lives Today*. New York: Summit.

Sklare, Marshall. 1978. "Jewish Acculturation and American Jewish Identity." In *Jewish Life in America: Historical Perspectives*, ed. Gladys Rosen, 167–88. New York: Ktav and Institute of Human Relations.

Smidt, Corwin E. 2013. *American Evangelicals Today*. Lanham: Rowman and Littlefield.

Smith, Christian, and Robert Fairs. 2005. "Socioeconomic Inequality in the American Religious System: An Update and Assessment." *Journal for the Scientific Study of Religion* 44(1): 95–104.

Smith, Greg, and Alan Cooperman. 2013. *What Happens When Jews Intermarry?* Pew Research Center, November 12, www.pewresearch.org/fact-tank/2013/1/12/what-happens-when-jews-intermarry.

Smith, Tom W. 1991. *Counting Flocks and Lost Sheep: Trends in Religious Preference Since World War II*. Rev. ed. Chicago: University of Chicago Press.

——. 2009. *Religious Switching Among American Jews*. New York: American Jewish Committee.

Sowell, Thomas. 1981. *Ethnic America: A History*. New York: Basic Books.

Sporlein, Christoph, Elmar Schlueter, and Fran van Tubergen. 2014. "Ethnic Intermarriage in Longitudinal Perspective: Testing Structural and Cultural Explanations in the United States, 1880–2011." *Social Science Research* 43 (January): 1–15.

Stark, Rodney. 1999. "Secularization, R.I.P." *Sociology of Religion: A Quarterly Review* 60(3): 249–73.

——, and William Sims Bainbridge. 1987. *A Theory of Religion*. New Brunswick, NJ: Rutgers University Press.

Swatos, William H., Jr. 1981. "Beyond Denominationalism? Community and Culture in American Religion." *Journal for the Scientific Study of Religion* 20(3): 217–27.

——, and Paul M. Gustafson. 1992. "Meaning, Continuity, and Change." In *Twentieth-Century World Religious Movements in Neo-Weberian Perspective*, ed. William H. Swatos Jr., 3–20. Lewiston, NY: Mellen.

Tajfel, Henri. 1981. *Human Groups and Social Categories: Studies in Social Psychology*. Cambridge: Cambridge University Press.

Thompson, Jennifer A. 2014. *Jewish on Their Own Terms: How Intermarried Couples Are Changing American Judaism*. New Brunswick, NJ: Rutgers University Press.

Tighe, Elizabeth, David Livert, Melissa Barnett, and Leonard Saxe. 2010. "Cross-Survey Analysis to Estimate Low-Incidence Religious Groups." *Sociological Methods and Research* 39(1): 56–82.

Turner, Bryan S. 1993. "Talcott Parsons, Universalism, and the Educational Revolution: Democracy Versus Professionalism." *British Journal of Sociology* 44(1): 1–24.

U.S. Census Bureau. 1958. *Current Population Reports: Population Characteristics*. Series P-20, no. 79. Washington, DC.

——. 2008. *Statistical Abstract of the United States*. Washington, DC.

Van der Eijk, Cees, and Mark N. Franklin. 2009. *Elections and Voters*. Basingstoke: Palgrave Macmillan.

Wald, Kenneth D. 2003. *Religion and Politics in the United States*. 4th ed. Lanham: Rowman and Littlefield.

Walzer, Michael. 1986. "Is Liberalism (Still) Good for the Jews?" *Moment* 11:13–19.

Warner, R. Stephen. 1998. "Approaching Religious Diversity: Barriers, Byways, and Beginnings." *Sociology of Religion: A Quarterly Review* 59 (3): 193–215.

Waxman, Chaim I. 1980. *Single-Parent Families: A Challenge to the Jewish Community*. New York: National Jewish Family Center of the American Jewish Committee.

——. 1992. "All in the Family: American Jewish Attachment to Israel." *Studies in Contemporary Jewry*, vol. 8: *A New Jewry? America Since the Second World War*, ed. Peter Y. Medding, 134–49. New York: Oxford University Press.

——. 2001. *Jewish Baby Boomers: A Communal Perspective*. Albany: State University of New York Press.

Weber, Max. 1946. *From Max Weber: Essays in Sociology*, ed. H. H. Gerth and C. Wright Mills. New York: Oxford University Press.

——. 1978 [1922]. *Economy and Society*. Berkeley: University of California Press.

——. 1991 [1922]. *The Sociology of Religion*. Boston: Beacon.

Weisberg, Herbert F. 2012. "Reconsidering Jewish Presidential Voting Statistics." *Contemporary Jewry* 32(3): 215–36.

——, and Steven Greene. 2003. "The Political Psychology of Party Identification." In *Electoral Democracy*, ed. Michael B. MacKuen and George Rabinowitz, 83–124. Ann Arbor: University of Michigan Press.

Welch, Michael R., and John Baltzell. 1984. "Geographic Mobility, Social Integration, and Church Attendance." *Journal for the Scientific Study of Religion* 23(1): 75–91.

Wilcox, Clyde, Ted G. Jelen, and David C. Leege. 1993. "Religious Group Identifications: Toward a Cognitive Theory of Religious Mobilization." In *Rediscovering the Religious Factor in American Politics*, ed. David C. Leege and Lyman A. Kellstedt., 72–99. New York: Routledge.

Wilder, Esther I. 1996. "Socioeconomic Attainment and Expressions of Jewish Identification, 1970 and 1990." *Journal for the Scientific Study of Religion* 35(2): 109–27.

Windmueller, Steven. 2003. *Are American Jews Becoming Republicans? Insights Into Jewish Political Behavior*. Jerusalem Viewpoints, no. 50. Jerusalem: Jerusalem Center for Public Affairs.

Wistrich, Robert. 2010. *A Lethal Obsession: Anti-Semitism from Antiquity to the Global Jihad*. New York: Random House.

Woocher, Jonathan. 2005. "Sacred Survival Revisited: American Jewish Civil Religion in the New Millennium." In *The Cambridge Companion to American Judaism*, ed. Dana Evan Kaplan, 283–297. New York: Cambridge University Press.

Woodhead, Linda. 2007. "Gender Differences in Religious Practice and Significance." In *The Sage Handbook of the Sociology of Religion*, ed. James A. Beckford and N. Jay Demerath III, 550–70. Los Angeles: Sage.

Woods, Michael. 2009. "Rural Geography: Blurring Boundaries and Making Connections." *Progress in Human Geography* 33(6): 849–58.

Wuthnow, Robert. 1988. *The Restructuring of American Religion*. Princeton: Princeton University Press.

——. 2003. "Studying Religion, Making It Sociological." In *Handbook of the Sociology of Religion*, ed. Michelle Dillon, 16–30. Cambridge: Cambridge University Press.

———. 2004. *Saving America? Faith-Based Services and the Future of Civil Society*. Princeton: Princeton University Press.

———. 2007. *After the Baby Boomers: How Twenty- and Thirty-Somethings Are Shaping the Future of American Religion*. Princeton: Princeton University Press.

Xie, Yu, and Kimberley Goyette. 1997. "The Racial Identification of Biracial Children with One Asian Parent: Evidence from the 1990 Census." *Social Forces* 76(2): 547–70.

Young, Lawrence A., ed. 1997. *Rational Choice Theory and Religion: Summary and Assessment*. New York: Routledge.

INDEX

Soviet Union, Jewish emigration from, 28, 30, 38–39
Spatial and socioeconomic stratification: of black Protestants, 56, 58, 61, 67, 70, 71, 74, 77, 79; determinants of socioeconomic attainment, 72–79; educational attainment, 59–63; of evangelical Protestants, 56, 61, 71, 79; geography and spatial dispersion, 54–59; income levels, 63–72; of mainline Protestants, 53, 63, 67, 74, 77, 79; religion-class nexus, 51–54
Spatial dispersion. *See* Geography and spatial dispersion
Spiritual communities, 16
Spiritual leader-centered religious forms, 5
Spouse: religious identity of, *86–87*; religious switching and, 41
SSA. *See* Smallest space analysis
Structural and cultural changes, of Jews, 8–9, 16
Structure, of religious identification, 131–32; coefficient of alienation with, 112; facet theory with, 106–7; mapping sentence for, 107, *108*; research variables relating to, 107–8, 111, *113*, 119–20, 123, 126, 127, 129, 133, 195n3; SSA for, 107–8, *110*, 111
Study: of Jews, 22–24, 168–69; of micro factors, of religion, 172–73; of religious patterns, 166–67
Suburban sprawl, in meso and macro spheres, 180
Surveys: of Jewish population, 28–31, 191n2; *see also specific surveys*
Synagogue: attendance at, 15; membership in, 15, 113, 114, 115

Technology, in meso and macro spheres, 180–81
Theological and social barriers, to interfaith marriage, 82
Traditional religious institutions, 5, 9

Traits: of micro factors, of religion, 173; of sociodemographic characteristics, religious identification, and voting patterns, 151, 160
Transformation, of religion in America, 9
Trends, in American religious life, 10–12
Twentieth century, American Jewish liberalism in, 137, 140, 164
2004 presidential election: Jews and non-Jews in, 144–47, *145*; Kerry in, 144–46, 147–51, *157–58*, 159–61

Unaffiliated, 35, *35*, 151, 192n6
United States: immigration to, 2–3; Jewish population in, 28–30, 191n1
Universalism, 53
Urban and rural residence, spatial dispersion between, 56–58
Utility, religion and, 165

Variables: interpersonal instrumental perspective by, 120–25; of religious identification structure, 107–8, 111, *113*, 119–20, 123, 126, 127, 129, 133, 195n3; of socioeconomic attainment determinants, 72–73, 74, 193n4
Venue, with group identification, 104
Voting determinants, 137, 159–64
Voting patterns. *See* Jewish political orientation, voting patterns and; sociodemographic characteristics, religious identification, and voting patterns

WASP mainstream, 172
West: education in, 73; income in, 70–71; intermarriage in, 89, 94; spatial dispersion in, 55–56
White Protestants, 4, 12
Worldview, religion and, 165

Yiddish words, 19